Walking Fife, The Ochils, Tayside and the Forth Valley

Clan Walk Guides

Walking Fife,
The Ochils, Tayside
and the Forth Valley

Walking Scotland Series
Volume 21

Mary Welsh
and
Christine Isherwood

First published by Clan Books, 2012

ISBN 978 1 873597 37 8
Text and Illustrations
© Mary Welsh
and Christine Isherwood 2012

Clan Books
Clandon House
The Cross, Doune
Perthshire
FK16 6BE

Printed and bound in Great Britain by
Bell & Bain Ltd., Glasgow

Publisher's Note

With the publication of this volume and its companion, "Walking Ayrshire, Renfrewshire and Lanarkshire", the authors and publishers are celebrating the completion of the Walking Scotland Series. Each of the twenty-one volumes in the series aspires to offer for all those who walk for pleasure a balanced cross-section of expeditions ranging from leisurely strolls to challenging mountain ridges and summits.

This new volume maintains the tradition. It bestrides the two great estuaries of the Forth and the Tay, visiting the hills easily reached from Edinburgh, and the Lomond and Ochil ranges, which rise spectacularly from the lower-lying lands between the two major rivers. There is also a fine variety of rambles by the incomparable Fife coast, and many intriguing and peaceful places are discovered among the country parks, woodlands, rivers and lochs that abound throughout this distinctive and delightful landscape.

There will always be changes affecting the many paths and tracks in our series of guides, and it is our intention to re-visit each area in turn when a new printing of a volume is imminent, to reflect new access developments. In this way we shall maintain the accuracy of the venture, which has been widely welcomed as an indispensible companion for walkers seeking to discover and enjoy Scotland's unrivalled countryside.

The Authors' Golden Rules for Good, Safe Walking

- Wear suitable clothes and take adequate waterproofs.

- Walk in strong footwear; walking boots are advisable.

- Carry the relevant map and a compass and know how to use them.

- Carry a whistle; remember six long blasts repeated at one minute intervals is the distress signal.

- Do not walk alone, and tell someone where you are going.

- If mist descends, return.

- Keep all dogs under strict control. Observe all "No Dogs" notices – they are there for very good reasons.

In all volumes of the WALKING SCOTLAND series, the authors make every effort to ensure accuracy, but changes can occur after publication. Reports of such changes are welcomed by the publisher. Neither the publisher nor the authors can accept responsibility for errors, omissions or any loss or injury.

Contents

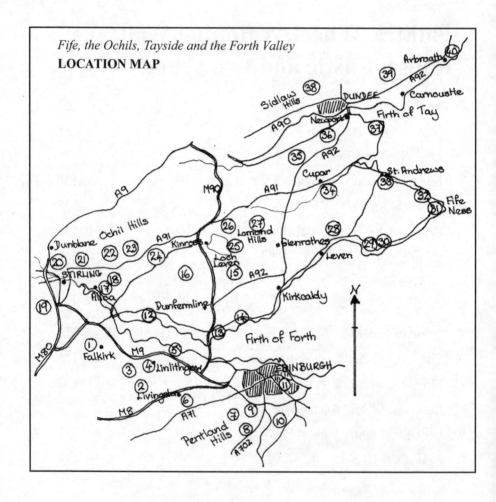

Fife, the Ochils, Tayside and the Forth Valley
LOCATION MAP

Walk 1

Falkirk Wheel, Antonine Wall, Rough Castle and two Canals

Park in the well-signed car park for visitors to the Falkirk Wheel, grid ref 854805. Access to the Wheel is signed from all major roads for miles around. If approaching by the A9, either from the centre of Falkirk or from the north, on reaching the central roundabout in Camelon, take the A803 west for about a mile, eventually passing under two railway overbridges. At the roundabout beyond, go left to reach the car park.

The spectacular **Falkirk Wheel** is located at Bonnybridge close to Falkirk. A millennium project, it links the Forth and Clyde and Union canals between Glasgow and Edinburgh and coast–to-coast across Scotland. The unique Wheel links the two canals with water levels 115ft/36m apart. This feat traditionally would need 11 locks. Attached to the Wheel at the top water level is an aqueduct with five huge 'loops'. This allows boats to enter and exit the Wheel.

The **Antonine Wall**, once the north-west frontier of the Roman Empire, was constructed between AD142 and 144. It stretched for 37 miles/60km and formed a solid barrier from the River Forth to the River Clyde. Its purpose was to

The Falkirk Wheel

control the movement of people and goods and also for defence. The ditch is the most obvious feature with remains of a mound on the north side and the wall represented by another mound on the south side. These mounds provide wonderful walking.

A time spent exploring the site of **Rough Castle**, a Roman fort, is a must. Look for ramparts, pits which contained sharply pointed stakes for protection, humps and bumps where stone buildings once stood.

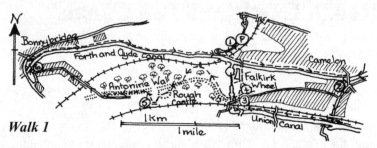

Walk 1

1 Leave by the end of the parking area, following the signs to the Falkirk Wheel, to climb a track to the side of the Forth and Clyde Canal, where you walk left. Pause to look right to see the magnificent Falkirk Wheel and save your visit until later. Carry on along the sturdy towpath past moored narrow boats. The houses to your left lie behind a wall and are mainly hidden from view by bushes and a hedge. On the right, beyond the cut, a pasture slants quite steeply upwards. Eventually the houses end and there are pastures on either side and here to the left you might spot a group of roe deer. Look for siskins enjoying the 'nuts' on the alders and yellowhammers calling from the depth of the bushes. After a mile on this pleasing way you arrive at Lock 16 at Camelon. Turn right onto the road bridge and look on along the cut which descends through a series of locks. Beyond the bridge, bear right along the other side of the canal. In a few steps set off, left, up a metalled path which curves pleasingly through a green with scattered trees, and the famous Union Inn away to your right, soon to join busy Glenfuir Road.

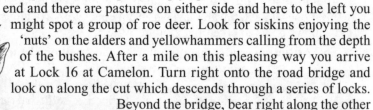

2 Continue up the road, ignoring all left and right turns. Pass under the railway bridge and take the signed track on the left side of the road, that climbs

Roe deer

8

through fine deciduous woodland to come to the side of the Union Canal, where you curve round right on the towpath. In early spring look for a profusion of white butterbur carpeting the woodland floor. Stroll the lovely way now with woodland on either side of the waterway. Look for goosanders just before you, and the canal, cross high above a road. The Cut then continues parallel with the railway, both sharing the best way through the countryside high above the houses in the valley. Go on to cross a narrow lane, where you turn left and then right to join the towpath once more. Stride on to reach two locks, which bring the waterway down a dramatic drop in the countryside.

3 Wind round, right, with the towpath, now railed, to enter the 590ft/180m Rough Castle tunnel. (Take heed of the notice, which says that it is closed from dusk to dawn.) You might be lucky to see a boat passing through it – at five miles an hour. As you emerge from the tunnel you have an amazing stretch of the canal ahead, channelled all the way to the famous wheel. Have your camera ready here. You can walk for a short way along the side of the water then you must return and drop down a paved curving track. After about 66ft/20m turn sharp right onto a path ascending from it and continue upwards to cross, right, over the top of the tunnel, from where there is a magnificent view of the Wheel.

4 Very soon take a short, narrow path up through the trees to join a good track through more of the lovely woodland and walk right. Look left as you go for a low raised mossy ridge, part of the Antonine Wall. Carry on until you reach a cross of tracks. Here go ahead as directed for the 'Wall and Rough Castle', coming close beside the railway once more. Look for goldfinches on willows as you go. The path brings you to a 'stile' beyond which you join a raised area to walk on the superb mossy way through scattered trees. This raised way is where the soil was thrown up when the ditch was dug or the grass-covered wall itself. Stroll along this raised area to a plaque on a low stone plinth and turn left over the ditch and up onto the site of the fort. There is little to see of stone work but the grassy ramparts and defensive post holes are very evocative of times long ago. Descend down the slope, right, towards the Rowan Tree Burn, noticing more fine ramparts on the right as you go.

5 Cross the plank bridge over the burn and walk left and almost immediately, right, up a narrow path onto a hill to rejoin the Antonine Wall. Follow the path to reach a small car park. Do not join the road here but continue along beside the wall on the left, keeping well above a row of small circular ponds. On reaching a walled wood, take the stile onto

the road and go on down hill. It is a delight at first. Go on past the fine gates to Bonnyside House. Then hurry as quickly as you can past a recycling and waste disposal business on the left and more waste material on the right. Continue past some new houses and carry on until the road swings left uphill.

6 Leave the road and head down, right, to a small burn and walk a raised, wrought-iron railed path above the cobbled bed of the hurrying water as it passes through a tunnel under the Forth and Clyde Canal. The path is not lit and near the middle it can be worryingly dark – use your torch if you have one. Emerge into the daylight to join a busy road at Bonnybridge and walk left, climbing the pavement to reach a lifting bridge over the Forth and Clyde Canal. Here walk left before the bridge onto the towpath beside the broad canal. Carry on, enjoying the mallards and the swans and then a considerable stretch of the pleasant countryside until you reach the footbridge across the Cut to visit the Falkirk Wheel Visitor Centre. Then return over the bridge and turn left to follow the signs for the car park.

Sand Martins

Practicals

Type of walk: *There is much to see on this very interesting walk. Generally good paths and tracks.*

Distance: 6–7 miles/9.5–11.3 km
Time: 4 hours
Maps: OS Explorer 349/Landranger 65

Walk 2

Torphichen

Park at the Community Centre at Torphichen village, grid ref 968726. Access this by the A801 and the B8047.

The superb tower and two transepts are all that remain of the dramatic **Torphichen Preceptory**, built in the 13th century, and associated with the Knights Hospitaller of the Order of St John of Jerusalem. Only two such establishments were maintained in Britain, the other being in London. To visit there is a small entrance fee. It is open summer weekends and bank holidays, 1–5pm.

Cairnpapple Henge, a splendid complex site, was in use for over a thousand years from around 2800BC. Look for the arc of seven holes where once Neolithic cremated human remains were placed. At a later period standing stones were arranged in an oval and a ditch was dug outside the oval. All trace of bones has gone, destroyed by the acid soil. Later still a cairn was built within the henge. A much bigger cairn was built later probably during the Bronze Age. Later more graves were dug in the Iron Age. The current site, a magnificent reconstruction, represents the original Bronze Age cairn.

Torphichen Preceptory

11

Walk 2

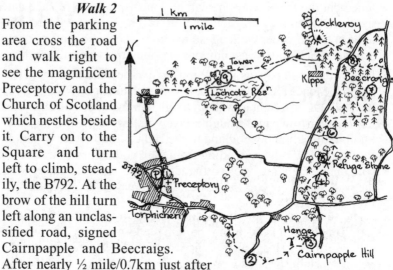

1 From the parking area cross the road and walk right to see the magnificent Preceptory and the Church of Scotland which nestles beside it. Carry on to the Square and turn left to climb, steadily, the B792. At the brow of the hill turn left along an unclassified road, signed Cairnpapple and Beecraigs. After nearly ½ mile/0.7km just after the point where the road bears a little left, look for an unmarked gate on the right. Beyond, walk up a wet grassy track, with a low wall to the left and a fence to the right. Eventually, the way is blocked by some aggressive gorse and you need to climb through the little wall where other walkers have gone before. Then continue up and up, with the track to your right. Remain in the pasture until you can go through a gate onto a road. Cross and wriggle through the gap in the rails at the side of the cattle grid opposite and stroll on.

2 Follow the good track beyond. The views are splendid and the way lined with fine beech on the left and rolling hills to the right. Stride the track as it winds left and climbs gently onto high grassland to reach the foot of a towering radio station and its related buildings. Curve right beside the transmitter and at the track end go through a gate. Look left to see what looks like a farm building (the small information centre) and head towards the fence in front of it. Keep along the fence to come to the entrance to Cairnpapple Henge. Walk the good path and then spend a wondrous time wandering around the splendidly restored prehistoric burial ground.

3 Return to the entrance and walk straight ahead over the pasture on an indistinct path to reach a flight of steps down to a gate and then more steps beyond to a minor road. Turn left and descend gradually. When half way along the crash barrier on your right, turn right down a short stretch of road to join a parallel road, which you cross to a wire fence across the track along which you continue. A notice apologises for the

fence but the farmer says he can no longer afford to replace gates to the track when they are stolen so often. The best way to cross seems to be at the left side. Walk ahead to climb a stile and then go on up the arrowed track with a vast number of young trees on either side.

4 Follow the good path as it descends to a valley and then wind right to climb the fence ahead by a stile. If you wish to climb Witch Craig Hill, turn left. Or turn right to walk to a sign naming the wood and here turn left on a narrow path through a lovely valley below the slopes of the knoll to the left and woodland to the right. Climb the easy path to the foot of the low ridge extending from the knoll. Pause by a ramshackle stile on the right and look to the left of it to see a sanctuary stone in the wall. This is one of the stones, which marked the boundary of the Preceptory at Torphichen.

5 Climb the little slope left onto the ridge and pause at the shelter, constructed with stones that you might find in the land all around. Some of the stones have letters on them and an information board tells you their geological history. A short way along the ridge is a plaque naming the hills you can see. Carry on the lovely way and then descend the end of the ridge to join a path continuing parallel with a wall to your right and with more young trees to the left. At the cross wall, at the foot of the path, turn left and follow it along to reach a complex stile on the right, over the wall and a wet area.

6 Turn left and soon bear right, up beside a plantation on the left to go through a gate where there is a sign welcoming you to Beecraigs Country Park. Cross the end of a narrow track and go ahead along a wide track through sitka spruce, following a large signpost directing you to Balvormie. Ignore two narrow paths off to the left, and press on up passing through large stands of magnificent Scots pine, until you reach a wide T-junction. Turn left here and continue until you come to a cross of tracks, a lane and the edge of a large meadow.

7 Take the grassy track ahead into the pleasing meadowland. At a Y-junction, bear right and curve left with it where it joins a path coming in on the right. Stroll this pleasing way over the brow and then go down, slightly left, towards two large stone circular barbeque stations, with an open sided shelter between. Keep to the left of all three and go on to reach a signpost and toilets. Go left into the forest for about 330ft/100m where the path swings right. In another 330ft/100m there is a waymark arrow (pale blue) indicating a well-made forest path on the right. Go along here, across a boardwalk, and on to the road. Cross with care and follow the path ahead through the trees. Go through

a small gate on your right and walk up the broad grassy path to the summit of Cockleroy. Here you are rewarded for the easy climb by a magnificent all-round view, with a view indicator to help you interpret it. The summit is surrounded by crags, especially on the western and northern sides, and was the site of a fort in ancient times. In spring listen for the call of a green woodpecker from the woods below.

8 Return down the grassy path, but before you reach the trees look for a less obvious path on the right running parallel to the wall. Walk along this below the crags of Cockleroy until you come to a gate in a fence. Go through and carry on straight ahead, then tending slightly left, to descend a long gently sloping field to a gate in the far corner, where there is a signpost. Go through the gate and turn right, on a wide obvious track, heading for Torphichen. The delightful track takes you on through thriving grassland with more hills away to right and left. Soon Lochcote reservoir comes into view. After nearly a mile walk through a gate into a thinly wooded area to pass a picturesque remnant of Loch Cote Castle.

9 The track takes you downhill to pass a fine house up on your right. Follow its very good access track that goes on descending to come close to the reservoir where you might spot goldeneye and tufted duck. Pass the dam with its manicured grass and continue to a wrought iron gate across the track. Go through the two kissing gates to the left side of the gate and walk on soon to curve left and then right along a rather wet farm track. At the farm buildings, turn left to join the narrow lane, left, which descends to a little valley with small Brunton Burn flowing through it. Beyond the bridge, climb towards the houses at Torphichen. At the top of the hill cross the road and go ahead to reach the Community Centre where you have parked.

Green Woodpecker

Practicals

Type of walk: *Delightful, full of contrasts, with several points of interest along the way.*

Distance:	6½ miles/10.5km
Time:	4 hours
Maps:	OS Explorer 349/Landranger 65

Walk 3

Muiravonside Country Park

Park in Muiravonside, grid ref 963755. Access this from the B825, which runs from Linlithgow to Avonbridge. The clearly signed Country Park entrance is 1 mile/2 km east of the roundabout junction with A801.

   After World War 2 (1945) the estate, owned by the Stirling family of Falkirk, went into decline. It was acquired by Falkirk Council in 1978. It covers an area of 170 acres, which is rich in historical, industrial and wildlife interests. There are **wonderful walks along the River Avon**, which now form part of the 'River Avon Heritage Trail', with links to the Union Canal and the wider countryside. There are approximately four miles of footpaths within the Park, ample car parking, a visitor centre, the Steading Café and three picnic areas. The old mansion has been demolished but lots of other bits and pieces remain.

Muiravonside Aqueduct

The **Avon Aqueduct** is 810ft/250m long and 86ft/26m high. It is the longest and tallest in Scotland and the second tallest in Britain. It was constructed after a design by Thomas Telford. There are 12 arches and the water is carried in a cast iron trough. There is a towpath along both sides. It is dramatic but can't be viewed from a distance.

Walk 3

1 Leave the parking area and follow the signpost for the Visitor Centre. Opposite the latter is the café. Walk round behind it to take steps down to cross a green and come beside the River Avon. Walk right, following the Heritage Trail towards the village of Avonbridge. The path leads you high above the Avon once you enter the forest and then easy paths take you steadily downhill to just above the fine river. Splendid woodland stretches up to the right where wild daffodils grow in spring and pleasing hedged fields stretch away on the opposite bank. Then you emerge onto a large field beside the tree-lined river. Stroll to the end and at the blue arrowed path that continues, turn right to climb a path up through the splendid woodland. At a T-junction turn left to walk a short path to join another path. Here turn sharp right. A short way along an easy-to-miss indistinct path drops left for a few steps to join a path at the edge of the forest where you stride on right to join a road.

2 Turn left and head on to cross a small burn. Immediately beyond take a narrow path on the right heading on through the forest. The pleasing way takes you through woodland, parallel with the burn, then continues so high above it that it is out of sight in its narrow deep ravine. The now mossy walled way moves out beside arable land. At the staggered cross of tracks, go ahead on the highest track. Soon through the trees to your left you glimpse the superb aqueduct that carries the Union Canal and then you reach the well constructed long flight of wooden steps that lead up to the canal. Many walkers will want to ascend the steps to see the magnificent structure and maybe walk along it and then return.

3 Then a decision needs to be made whether to descend the many steps and carry on beside the River Avon. Or you may wish to make a small loop with a challenge in the middle. If so walk on along the canal from the end of the aqueduct. Notice across the river a mossy covered dry

16

dock, still with the shell of a boat within it, equally moss-covered. Continue to the first bridge. Just before it comes the challenge in the shape of small stone steps, with some missing, which take you steeply up to the road over the bridge. There is a tiny gap in the wall onto the road or you may prefer to climb the wooden rails. Turn left, cross the bridge and take the entrance, on the left, back into the Park. This returns you to the staggered cross of tracks where you turn left on the highest track. Stride ahead to come to the foot of the long flight of wooden steps up to the aqueduct, again.

4 Continue along the riverside this time and then, on reaching the last of several buildings, turn right to take the upper of two paths. Climb steadily up through trees and at the top bear left to descend steps and carry on along a level path still well above the river. Ascend steps again to pass through the middle of a small cemetery. Follow the path and view the river, to your left, which lies very far below, to arrive at an interesting doocot well used by a flock of white doves. Drop down beside the children's playground and turn right into the courtyard with the café on the left and the information centre and toilets to the right. Then take the footpath or track beyond, which leads back to the parking area.

Doves

Practicals

Type of walk: *Very pleasant. Through woodland, by the river, and along the canal, all on good paths or tracks.*

Distance: 3 miles/5km
Time: 2 hours
Maps: OS Explorer 349/Landranger 65

Walk 4

Linlithgow Loch

Park in a layby on the A706, grid ref 976758. This lies on the south side of the road just west of a canal building.

Linlithgow Palace was built for James I in the 15th century after the town was partially destroyed in a great fire in 1424. Mary Queen of Scots was born there in 1542. In 1746 it became a ruin when the army of the Duke of Cumberland set it on fire. It has been actively conserved since the 19th century and today is managed and maintained by Historic Scotland. The site is open to visitors throughout the year.

A church stood on the site where **St Michael's** now stands and was mentioned in a charter in the 12th century. It was dedicated or re-dedicated in 1242. After fire damage in the 15th century it was more or less rebuilt. It has had a chequered career. Edward I of England used it as a military storehouse. During the 17th century it was used as a timber store and later Cromwell stabled his horses here. There was once a stone crown on the tower, but this was removed in 1821. The modern crown, a metal one, which represents the Crown of Thorns, was put in position in 1964.

Linlithgow Loch was formed when a great lump of ice broke off a retreating glacier during the Ice Age. This was covered with glacial debris, forming the present day soil. The ice melted and left a great hollow (a kettle-hole) and water filled this creating the loch.

Linlithgow Palace

1 From the layby go through a purpose-built gap onto the Union Canal towpath and turn left, with the delightful waterway to your right. Continue on soon to pass under a narrow stone bridge. Beyond, deciduous woodland slopes up on the right and in a large field, to the left, common gulls often feed. In the hedgerow look for bullfinches, these colourful birds brighten the way. Continue on with the finely kept greens of the golf course on the opposite bank to pass under another bridge. Eventually you pass houses down below the hedgerow from where greenfinches call. Carry on to pass under a road bridge. Watch out for your first glimpse of the magnificent Linlithgow Palace and St Michael's Church, across the countryside and houses to your left. Pass under another road bridge and press on a short way to reach, on the right side of the canal, the Linlithgow Union Canal Centre, with several narrow boats pulled up in front of the building. To your left is a well-preserved doocot.

2 Ahead is another bridge but, before this, leave the towpath, cross the road leading up to the bridge, to join Station Road and follow it as it drops down left through a barrier. Curve down the walled traffic-free way to pass under a railway bridge. Wind left, descending to the main street passing Platform Three restaurant and pub on the corner. Turn right to use the island to cross the busy street and walk left, past many interesting shops, and enjoying the baronial architecture. At The Cross, curve round half way to climb up Kirkgate. As you ascend notice the small plaques on the right wall that list all the kings and queens that reigned after Mary Queen of Scots, who was born at the Palace. Go through the 16th century Fore Entrance Gateway to reach St Michael's Church on the right. Inside the lovely building you feel as if you are in a beautiful cathedral.

3 Walk ahead from the church to descend a curving path along the side of the Peel. Turn acute left to start your walk, clockwise, round the splendid Linlithgow Loch. Pass through a low wall. (Toilets are very difficult to find and in short supply in the town, but when you have passed through the wall and reached the first seat, a path goes off left then up a few steps to a

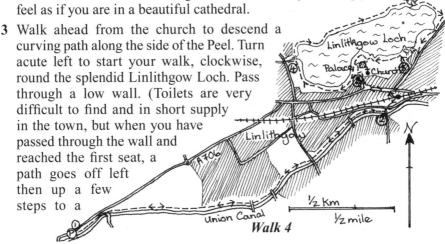

Walk 4

19

toilet block – 10p fee.) From now on
the path winds round the edge of
the loch where you will spot many
birds including large numbers of swans,
coots, tufted ducks, great crested grebes,
goldeneye, moorhens, mallards
and little grebes.

4 Continue on beside willows
that edge the loch and then
cross the outflow and wind
right. Soon the houses are
left behind and the slopes
to your left are clad with
trees and bushes. Reeds
colonise the edge of the
water. For most of the way
on this walk, you will have

Great crested grebes

had some splendid views of the magnificent palace and the church,
a view that is considered one of the great Scottish sights, and one of
which you will want to take pictures. Just before you reach a road, take
a kissing gate on your right to continue along the pleasing way. This
path leads you on along the opposite side of the loch, towards the Peel
and the Palace. Wind on round and then up a rising path to join a road.
Walk right for a short way and then take an interesting ginnel on the
right, signposted 'Peel and Loch ' to rejoin the lochside path.

5 Continue left past a children's playground and then a boat stage and
curve round the Peel to meet your outward path. Ascend left to St
Michael's, go through Fore Gate and descend Kirkgate. Retrace your
steps left, cross the road at the island and bear right for a few steps
and climb up Station Road to join the canal and walk right. Enjoy this
two-mile-and-a bit-walk to reach the parking area by the long building.

Practicals

Type of walk: *Full of interest. Good paths and tracks throughout
the walk.*

Distance: 7 miles/11.2km

Time: 4 hours

Maps: OS Explorer 349/Landranger 65

Walk 5

Blackness Castle and Wester Shore Wood

Park beside the Firth of Forth at Blackness, grid ref 051801. To your right, when facing the Firth, you have the church, the inn and a toilet block.

In the 1440s Sir George Crichton, Admiral of Scotland, built **Blackness Castle** on a basalt promontory projecting into the Firth of Forth, as a tower-house home. But his family were not allowed to enjoy it for long. James II seized it soon after, retaining it in Crown ownership and using it as a garrison fortress and state prison. In spite of its walls being thickened and heightened, like several other castles in Scotland, it did not withstand Cromwell's onslaught in the 17th century. It was finally abandoned during the 1914-1918 war. In the 1920s and 30s it was restored by the Office of Works. Today the castle is open to visitors for a small fee.

1 From the parking area walk east towards the castle and with the Firth to your left. You may wish to visit the impressive, sombre castle at the start of your walk or at the end. Then take the kissing gate right, at the outside edge of the gateway to the castle, to take steps and a short walk, leading to the beach from where you can see the two dramatic *Blackness Castle*

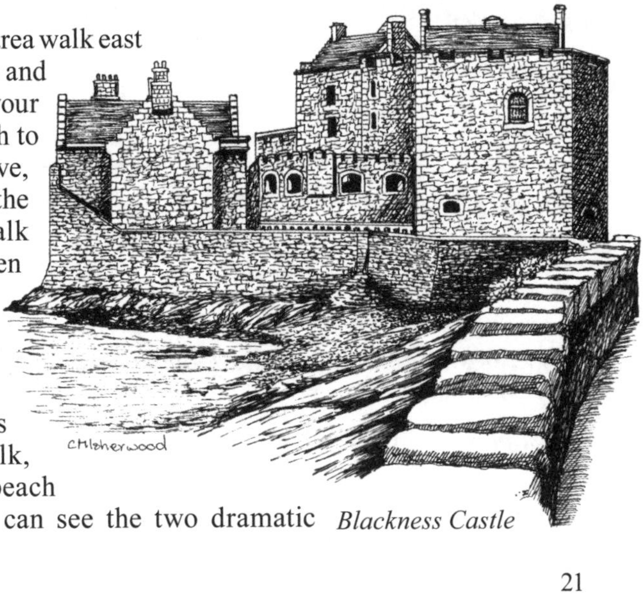

CHlzherwood

21

bridges across the Forth. Walk on round the huge sandy bay to reach winding Black Burn heading towards the shore and walk inland beside it to cross a footbridge. Beyond, take a metal gate on the right to walk a good reinforced track into mature woodland, keeping parallel with the low walled shore.

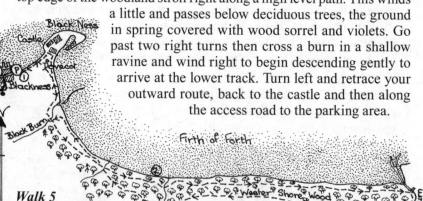

Shelduck

2 Ignore two right turns and carry on below the fine trees. In spring, listen as you go for robin, chaffinch and blackbird. After nearly a mile you continue through young deciduous woodland and in spring this is where you will hear warblers calling to attract a mate and establish a territory. At a T-junction do not go left over a burn and through gates, but bear right on the track and begin to climb gently. As you near the top edge of the woodland stroll right along a high level path. This winds a little and passes below deciduous trees, the ground in spring covered with wood sorrel and violets. Go past two right turns then cross a burn in a shallow ravine and wind right to begin descending gently to arrive at the lower track. Turn left and retrace your outward route, back to the castle and then along the access road to the parking area.

Walk 5

Practicals

Type of walk: *Very pleasant woodland walk, with a fine castle to explore if time.*

Distance: 4 miles/6.5km
Time: 2 hours
Maps: OS Explorer 349/ Landranger 65

Walk 6

Almondell and Lin's Mill Aqueduct

Park in the large parking area (northern), grid ref 091696. To access this, leave Edinburgh by the M8. Exit at Junction 1 to take the A89, west. At the first roundabout continue on the A89 and then take the second left turn. Go under the M8 and the railway bridge and continue ahead to the parking area.

The **Union Canal** follows the 73m contour throughout its 31.5 miles length, making locks unnecessary. The Millennium Link restored both the Union and the Forth and Clyde Canals and saw the two canals joined at the Falkirk end of the Union Canal, in the year 2000, by means of the Falkirk Wheel. The canal was once known as the Edinburgh and Glasgow Union Canal and, after joining the Forth and Clyde Canal at Falkirk, provided a through route between Scotland's two major cities.

A good place to stop for a break is the grassy area close by **Lin's Mill Aqueduct** see point 5. This aqueduct is the most spectacular of three carrying the Union Canal even though it is the smallest. It crosses over the River Almond in five arches, 75 ft/23m above the

Nasmith's Bridge, Almondell

23

river. William Lin who owned the nearby mill was the last person to die of the plague in Scotland. No one would help his wife bury him, so she dragged his body in a sack into the woods for burial. Lin's Mill is now privately owned.

The **feeder stream**, or leat, allows water from Cobbinshaw Reservoir on the northern side of the Pentland Hills, to keep the canal topped up.

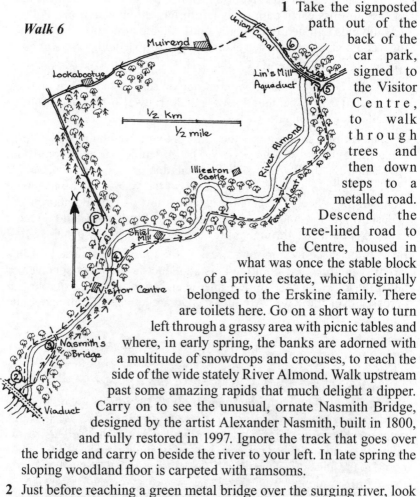

Walk 6

1 Take the signposted path out of the back of the car park, signed to the Visitor Centre, to walk through trees and then down steps to a metalled road. Descend the tree-lined road to the Centre, housed in what was once the stable block of a private estate, which originally belonged to the Erskine family. There are toilets here. Go on a short way to turn left through a grassy area with picnic tables and where, in early spring, the banks are adorned with a multitude of snowdrops and crocuses, to reach the side of the wide stately River Almond. Walk upstream past some amazing rapids that much delight a dipper. Carry on to see the unusual, ornate Nasmith Bridge, designed by the artist Alexander Nasmith, built in 1800, and fully restored in 1997. Ignore the track that goes over the bridge and carry on beside the river to your left. In late spring the sloping woodland floor is carpeted with ramsoms.

2 Just before reaching a green metal bridge over the surging river, look ahead to see an attractive narrow leat, a feeder stream for the Union Canal. Start to cross the metal bridge and half way over pause to look

24

upstream to see a splendid flaring viaduct. Walk on to the end of the bridge to look for the water of the leat channelled beneath your feet. Then wind left to walk with the leat to your right, just after it has emerged from under a small stone bridge. To your left a wide green sward stretches to the riverside and fine trees cover the slope to your right. Continue until you reach Nasmith Bridge again having made a pleasing loop.

3 Here turn acute right up a steepish metalled track. Watch out for where an easy-to-miss earth path leads left through rhododendrons. Follow it as it winds left, gently climbing until you are almost on the edge of the woodland, beyond which extends a vast arable field. The river now lies far down, almost out of sight. The track eventually narrows to a path and descends quite steeply to the top of steps. These are railed and descend to reach a path. Ahead is a fine suspension bridge over the River Almond, which you ignore. To your right the feeder for the canal emerges once more from beneath a culvert.

4 Walk right along the pleasing path with the leat flowing sweetly to your right. The hedged way on one side and the woodland on the other are full of small birds. Continue on this lovely way to pass through a gate. Cross a narrow lane and climb a stile, signed to Lin's aqueduct and continue on the excellent path beside the little stream of water. Carry on to where the leat is soon culverted below a steeply

Bullfinch

sloping knoll. The path continues through deciduous woodland to come beside the leat once again. Press on to cross stiles or kissing gates on either side of farm tracks as they pass over the feeder stream on more stone bridges. The path is railed where it comes close, at one point, to the edge of a deep drop to the River Almond below. Look left to see Lin's Aqueduct high above the trees, carrying the Union Canal. Eventually you reach, on your right, a steep flight of steps that needs to be climbed to arrive at a lane above. At the top turn left to descend the quiet way then bear right to the side of the Union Canal.

5 Here the feeder stream finally emerges to complete its job of supplying water to the canal. There is a large grassy area, between the Cut and the leat, with seats, and flowers under the hedge. Here, too, people bring their kayaks to set off along the waterway. If you use one of the seats to enjoy the scene, afterwards return to the lane and stroll on under superb Lin's Mill Aqueduct. There is a long flight of steps down from the green to the tunnel but these are quite arduous. Once through the tunnel ascend a similar flight of steps to attain the towpath. Turn right to walk across the magnificent aqueduct, seen earlier from the path beside the feeder stream. If you have a good head for heights, look down to the River Almond still rushing on its way to the sea and still foaming over rapids.

6 Carry on along the towpath soon to pass through more arable land. Then look right to see two enormously long viaducts, with innumerable arches, the railway making good use, as did the canal, of the easiest route across the countryside, between large conurbations. Before the next bridge over the Cut, join a farm track and go ahead to cross the bridge. Walk along the quiet metalled lane for nearly a mile, passing Muirend cottage, Lookabootye, and the entrance to the TA Centre at Drumshoreland. At the crossroads, turn left and walk the leafy lane for another ½ mile/1km to the car park.

Snowdrops and crocuses

Practicals

Type of walk: *Very interesting and enjoyable. The long path beside the feeder stream is a joy to walk.*

Distance: 6 miles/10km

Time: 3–4 hours

Maps: OS Explorer 350/Landranger 65

Walk 7

Threipmuir and Harlaw Reservoirs

Park in the car park for Threipmuir Reservoir, grid ref 167639. Access this, if approaching from the direction of Currie, by taking the signed left turn before the roundabout at Balerno. Continue ahead up the road and where it turns right, go on ahead along the quiet, hedge-lined no through road to reach the signed car park on the left.

From 1843 to 1848 engineer James Jardine constructed **Threipmuir reservoir**. It was one of a network to supply Edinburgh with water. It lies on the course of the Bavelaw Burn in the Pentland Hills. Though it is no longer used as a water supply it does provide a very pleasing walk. The Threipmuir adds its water to **Harlaw Reservoir** and it discharges into Bavelaw Burn.

The **redshank** as its name implies has long red legs. It stands bobbing in sandpiper fashion, dipping its head and breast as if hinged.

Harlaw reservoir

27

When it takes wing it shows a white lower back and a distinctive broad white border to the wing. In flight it looks very black and white. It announces its presence by a triple call, a haunting lovely sound.

Walk 7

1 Leave the car park, right, and rejoin the quiet road and turn left and walk on with woodland on either side, where you might spot siskins overhead and hear chiffchaffs. Just before Redford Bridge, look over Bavelaw Marsh to see heron, lapwing and redshank and then cross the bridge over the end of Threipmuir reservoir. Continue uphill along the private (to vehicles) tarmacked way under an arch of tall beeches, with wide grass verges on either side. At the T-junction turn left and wind on round with the narrow road to go through a signposted gate onto the rolling slopes at the foot of the Pentland Hills.

2 Follow the good waymarked path out across the moorland, with Hare Hill to your right. Look for yellow pansies, milkmaids and kingcups as you go. This is a good cinder path; enjoy it as it winds through the valley. Watch for wheatears flitting about the way and listen for the bubbling calls of curlew as they fly overhead. Carry on along the gated way until you reach Green Cleugh. Here turn left and begin a steep climb, on a good path, beside the wall, on your left, to reach the lower heather slopes of Black Hill.

3 Follow the path beside the wall as it goes on, with the reservoir down to your left. The path is obvious but it has suffered erosion in places and will be muddy after heavy rain. It traverses the hill slope, descending imperceptibly for just over a mile. Where the wall turns down left the path does too, to a stile, which you cross. Go on over the bridge-cum-dam across a narrow arm of the reservoir. Turn left and walk beside the reservoir. Look for goosanders on the water and common sandpipers along the shore. Press on until the path takes you through a pleasing belt of Scots pine. Emerge from the trees and soon pause to look right to see a picturesque cottage, the original Threipmuir farm. Move over to the wall on your right and a short way along turn right

28

onto a delightful path with
more Scots pine to the
left. Soon you can see the
Harlaw reservoir through the
trees.

4 Wind on round the end
of the reservoir and
press on with pines to
the left and agricultural
land to the right to reach
the small, pleasing visitor centre
where there is a toilet. The track winds

Common sandpiper

left just before the centre, crosses a footbridge across the overflow and
this is the way you continue. Soon you may prefer to walk through the
pines nearer to the water, to your left, rather than the tarmacked way.
Emerge from the trees to see to your left, the weir between the two
reservoirs. Cross the track and continue on through pines and then join
a track and follow it as it winds left. Head on along the wide way with
the Threipmuir to your left. Where it winds right to a private gate, take
a narrow path continuing beside the water. A few steps along take a
gate on the right, walk up a path to the next gate and turn left onto the
track once more. Continue ahead to reach the car park.

Goosander

Practicals

Type of walk: *Great walk of contrasts. Some paths could be muddy
after rain. Wear or carry the right kind of outdoor wear, as the
winds, and the rain, can sweep fiercely down the hills.*

Distance: 7 miles/11.3km
Time: 4–5 hours
Maps: OS Explorer 344/Landranger 65

Walk 8

Turnhouse Hill, Carnethy Hill, Scald Law and Two Reservoirs

Park at Flotterstone Rangers/Information Centre, grid ref 233631. Access this from the A702 by a west turn for Flotterstone Inn. Go past the inn and continue for 200yds to park in the large car park.

The **Pentlands,** a narrow range of volcanic hills that are not as rugged as those found in the Highlands, stretch for about 20 miles/32km, running south-west from Edinburgh towards Biggar and the Upper Clydesdale. The fine hills, sculpted by glaciers and water, were then shaped by people over thousands of years. Several rivers begin in the hills, including the Water of Leith and the North Esk.

Glencorse Reservoir was built by Thomas Telford in 1821. Not far from the edge of the large stretch of water lie the submerged ruins of the chapel of St Katherine's on the Hope. The chapel was built

Glencorse reservoir

after Sir William St Clair won an encounter with the King, Robert the Bruce. The latter staked his Pentland Estate against the life of St Clair during a deer hunt. Fortunately St Clair's dogs brought down the white deer in question and at his relief for not forfeiting his life St Clair had the chapel built to mark the spot in the glen.

1 Leave the car park by a footpath that keeps to the left of the Ranger Centre. The way through the trees is a delight, with bluebells and pink purslane flowering below the pines in spring and summer. Carry on ahead until the path emerges from the trees onto the road. Continue on the tree-lined road where you might spot a bullfinch as it calls quietly from a young elm tree. At the signpost, turn left in the direction of Scald Law and then left as signed again. Cross the sturdy footbridge where the burn is lined with gorse. Follow the path as it winds round, right, of a little hillock. It then climbs before descending a steepish slope and continuing to pass through a gate.

2 Continue up the steep path to reach a shoulder of the hill where there is a fenced plantation and a convenient bent trunk of a sycamore where you can pause, get your breath and enjoy the view. Carry on up the clear path, passing the odd wind blown larch. The way levels for a bit here and there is a delightful view of Glencorse reservoir, seemingly set around with forest trees, far down the slopes to your right. The path then begins to climb steeply before reaching a badly eroded way. Eventually you get beyond the erosion and the path, now stony, winds left and is good to walk. Soon it becomes grassy

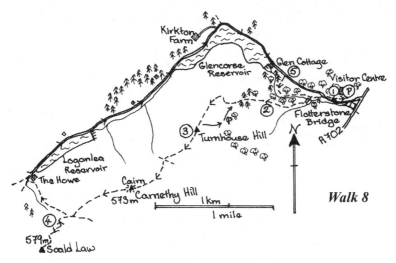

Walk 8

and reaches a faint junction of paths. Go on up, choosing the easiest way until you reach the summit of Turnhouse Hill with its small cairn (1670 ft/506m). Pause here to enjoy the superb view of the slopes ahead.

3 Carry on west down to the col before Carnethy Hill. There are paths going off on each side here, which could be used if you need to get down quickly. Cross the stile and climb the twisting stony path up the far side, which is not nearly as steep as it appears to be from Turnhouse Hill. In summer swifts and swallows swoop over the ground in search of flies, and you may see a kestrel hovering. The stone-cairned top of Carnethy Hill 1890ft/573m, the second highest of the Pentlands, is soon reached. Carry on down the far side, where after the first steep descent the slope levels for a while, then drops to the next col. The path is nowhere in doubt. Notice a good path running north here, your return route, but first cross the fence by a hurdle gate and climb the well-made zigzag path to the summit of Scald Law 1910ft/579m. This is the highest of the Pentland Hills and on a good day the view is superb. The summit is covered with low-growing bilberry and grass and is a tempting place to eat your lunch and sunbathe on a hot day.

Kestrel

4 Return downhill to the hurdle gate, go through and turn left to follow the good gravel path down into the valley. Wind round to the left of a white house, The Howe, to join a path coming in from the left and cross a burn on a culvert bridge. Join another path at a T-junction and turn right. Although the track soon becomes metalled there is almost no traffic and it is actually a very pleasant walk back through the valley. Almost immediately you walk along beside Loganlea Reservoir, then beside the Logan Burn. There is a wide verge of short flowery grass here, which is very pleasant underfoot. The burn gurgles over small waterfalls to your right; look out for dippers and grey wagtails. Then you reach Glencorse Reservoir, where you are likely to see a large flock of greylag geese. The road turns sharply right and continues under pine trees. Walk past the dam and Glen Cottage. Stroll on along the quiet lane with a mossy wall to your right beyond which are more splendid trees and take a signed gate on the right.

5 Descend the slope towards the lovely hollow seen from above. Go

on down the glen past a small area set aside as a wild flower garden and with a picnic table. This is a glorious sheltered area with some very fine trees and a lush understorey. Walk on past two disused buildings once part of the old filter beds of the Glencorse reservoir and go through a gate. Follow the winding path to reach the road. Turn right to return to the parking area. Or you may prefer at the signpost to ignore the glen walk and continue down the road and bear left to reach the car park.

Pink purslane

Practicals

Type of walk: *The climb to Turnhouse Hill is the most challenging on this exhilarating walk. After descending from the high level ridge the walk past the two reservoirs is a most pleasant contrast.*

Distance: 8 miles/13km
Time: 4 hours
Maps: OS Explorer 344/Landranger 66

Walk 9

Allermuir and Capelaw, Pentland Hills

Park in a reinforced area on the left side of the old road, grid ref 227680, just after a left turn, superseded by the very busy A720 City Bypass. To access this turn off the bypass at the slip road at Dreghorn roundabout, signed Dreghorn Ranges. Continue over the 'brow' and go on (as if to use the slip road to rejoin the A-road) but, a few yards along it, turn left and drive on to the unsigned parking area. This is marked with a P on the OS map but is a poor sort of parking area.

The Pentland Hills Regional Park came into being in 1984. Today most of the land is upland pasture, along with several plantations, some passed on this walk. The MOD has a rifle range at Castlelaw (not on this walk). Much of Edinburgh's water supply once came from reservoirs in the hills including Threipmuir, Harlaw and Glencorse, all walked beside in this book.

On many of the walks in this lovely area, **gorse** delights the eye by its great trusses of fragrant golden flowers. The hillsides are transformed, the sunlight reflecting off the petals and the air sweetly perfumed.

Pentland Hills from Capelaw

Gorse when in flower beautifies the valleys and the slopes in early summer but to some extent throughout the year.

1 From the parking area walk back to take the turn, now on your right, to pass through an iron kissing gate beside a large padlocked gate. Read, carefully, the information board just beyond, about the area being used for military training, especially as a rifle range, noting whether the red danger flag is flying. Press on through the next gate and carry on along the reinforced narrow track, edged with well-spaced young horsechestnut trees. When the metalling ends continue on the grass and dirt path, over the Dreghorn rifle range, which bears steadily right and winds round the corner of a plantation of spruce on your right. Carry on beside another plantation on the left and follow the track as it begins to climb steadily with ever-delightful views up the valley. Go through another kissing gate. Step across a little burn to reach a signpost beside a hut. Follow the sign for Castlelaw.

Walk 9

A720
(Edinburgh Bypass)
Dreghorn Junction
Dreghorn Rifle Ranges
Howden Burn
½ Km
½ mile
Allermuir Hill
↗493m
1453m
Capelaw Hill

2 Press on up the valley with the steep heather and bilberry slopes of Allermuir Hill to the left and the gorse covered slopes of Capelaw Hill to your right. You may see green hairstreak butterflies here in spring. About a mile from the start you reach a cross of tracks. Here take the left branch to walk a grassy trod, rising steadily and distinctly for ¼ mile/ 0.5km to cross the boundary fence to attain the trig point on the summit (1617ft/493m) of Allermuir. The views of Edinburgh are magnificent. Return down the path to the cross of tracks serenaded by skylarks in spring. You might also see golden plover, lapwing, roe deer and brown hares.

Green hairstreak butterfly

35

3 Cross your upward track and descend a short way to take the stile over a fence and then start your climb up to Capelaw. The path is grassy and rises easily, with another magnificent view of Edinburgh along the banks of the Firth of Forth with the Lomond Hills along the skyline. The climb is soon over and then the good grassy trod continues along the ridge. A little path right takes you to the rusting metal girder and struts that stand on the summit (1478 ft/454m).

4 Turn sharp right, keeping Arthur's Seat to your right and the two Forth bridges ahead, to begin your descent of this delightful hill. This is a slightly rougher path, a little eroded by horses. Pause often to enjoy the stunning views. Bear left round a spur of Capelaw and as the path descends make small detours to the left to avoid a couple of eroded slopes. Join a wide track and walk right with more exciting views ahead. Go through a gate and continue downhill with Arthur's Seat ahead and much closer.

5 Wind round right with the track beside a plantation on your left. Beyond, at a Y-junction, take the right branch and with another plantation to the left begin to descend on a grassy path through gorse. This brings you down to the hut and the signpost passed near the outset of the walk. Turn left and cross the little burn. Continue on your outward path. Pass between the two plantations and then bear left round the corner of the left plantation. Keep ahead on the wide track to reach the reinforced track that brings you to the kissing gate and then the information board. Go on through the iron kissing gate and turn left to return to the parking area.

Practicals

Type of walk: *Most enjoyable particularly when the gorse is in bloom. Steady climb to the cross of tracks. Steepish grassy path up to Allermuir Hill and a gentler ascent to Capelaw. Descent is made all on paths. The views are stunning. Do not attempt in the mist.*

Distance: 5 miles/8km

Time: 3–4 hours

Maps: OS Explorer 350/Landranger 66

Walk 10

Roslin Glen

Park in the large car park in Chapel Loan, grid ref 273632. This leads off the main street through Roslin, B7006, opposite the Original Roslin Hotel and Roslin Glen Hotel. The parking area lies on the right of the road just before you reach Rosslyn Chapel.

The splendidly decorated **Rosslyn Chapel** was founded in the 15th century on a hill above Roslin Glen. Nearby Roslin Castle and the Chapel are located close to the village of Roslin, Midlothian. The Chapel was founded by

Roslin Castle

37

the 1st Earl of Caithness. He used the designs of medieval architects, made available to him. It was a Roman Catholic church until the 1560 Scottish Reformation. Today, it is visited by the devoted readers of Dan Brown's *Da Vinci Code*, a worldwide best seller.

Roslin Castle was built in the 1330s, by Henry Sinclair the Earl of Orkney. The ruins stand high above a loop in the River North Esk, which in the castle's dramatic past protected it on three sides. Today it is approached by a precipitous bridge, which replaced earlier draw-bridges, then through a ruined gatehouse. From 1982–88 the east range was restored and the current owner now leases it as holiday accom-modation via the Landmark Trust.

1 Turn right out of the car park to visit the magnificent Rosslyn Chapel and the visitor centre. Then return a few steps along the road and drop left down a hedged lane to reach a cross of tracks and a sign-post. Turn left to walk a walled reinforced track, between two cem-eteries, which soon takes you over a walled bridge, with the River North Esk completely hidden deep down the immense drop of Roslin Glen, a stunning endless hollow completely filled with magnificent mature trees. Pause on the bridge for a dramatic view of Roslin Castle, the picturesque sandstone ruins perched seemingly precariously on the edge of this great ravine. Climb the slope to enjoy a little exploration. Then return back along the walled bridge and take the well-graded steps downhill, imme-diately on your left. At the foot turn left to pass under the bridge you have just crossed. Wind left and walk on with a fence to your right, with the river out of sight to your right.

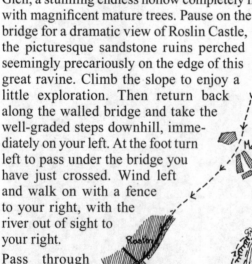

2 Pass through large patches of wild garlic below forest trees. Climb a small flight of steps with sanicle growing

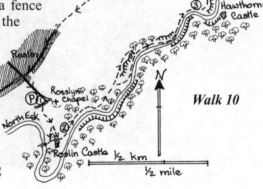

Walk 10

on either side of the flags. Bugle flowers, deeply purple, thrust their way through the wild garlic. Carry on up, ignoring all paths, on the right, which descend towards the bottom of the ravine. In spring and early summer the woodland is full of bird song. At a Y-junction take the right branch, keeping high, with yellow comfrey flowering to your right. Pass below a clump of ancient yews and bear right through bluebell woodland, the flowers filling the air with their perfume. Follow the path as it winds on quite steeply downhill with rough steps in places. Pause on a level part of the path to look across the river, visible now, with incredibly high sandstone cliffs dropping dramatically to the opposite shore of the fast flowing water. Here you might spot a cave. Wind round fallen trees or climb over or under them, as other walkers have done. Ignore the right turn down to river, where bluebells and pink purslane grow, and go ahead climbing gently.

Wild garlic

3 Go through an ancient fence where there was once a stile. Ignore the immediate left turn and go on to see, just below, an open area above more cliffs – take care here if you explore. Press on along the high level path and soon look across the ravine to spot Hawthornden Castle, a splendid sandstone mansion, best seen when the leaves are off the trees. Then the path begins to drop almost to the side of the river, easy to walk unless it is muddy after rain. The way climbs again and then descends close beside the river with a fenced pasture on the left. Now the river makes a wide bend and you walk round just above it to pass through a gate into Hewan Bank SSSI.

4 Here you might wish to go right to make a loop round the site of Maiden Castle, or turn left to climb several flights of well made steps first up a grassy slope and then into woodland. Follow the path as its winds, right, into trees. Continue climbing and wind left to ascend more steps, solid stone blocks, to carry on along the top of the bank to a well signposted gate onto a wide track.

5 Turn left and walk with a lovely slope to the right where many beech trees grace the drop. Enjoy the extensive views across the open

countryside, a pleasing contrast after your walk through the densely wooded Roslin Glen. Continue on the track through the buildings and dwellings of Mountmarle then pause beside the memorial to the Battle of Roslin, 24th February, 1303. It was here that a huge English army was defeated by a much smaller Scottish one. Carry on into Roslin and watch out for the left turn opposite the two hotels to return to the car park.

Great spotted woodpecker

Practicals

Type of walk: *All on paths, some reinforced, some steep, and some earthen –the latter muddy after heavy rain. It also continues on a good track and along a very quiet road.*

Distance: 5 miles/8km
Time: 3–4 hours
Maps: OS Explorer 344/Landranger 66

Walk 11

Arthur's Seat and Salisbury Crags

Park in the car park, named Meadowbank on the OS map, to the south of Edinburgh's St Margaret's Loch, grid ref 278741.

At 823ft/251m **Arthur's Seat** is Edinburgh's highest hill. It towers over Holyrood Park, a fine stretch of countryside in the centre of the city. The hill is part of an extinct volcano which erupted 340 million years ago and which has been eroded by a glacier, moving west to east. This is also how Salisbury Crags were formed.

The long monotonous 'reeling' song of the **grasshopper warbler** reveals its presence much more than its rather dull plumage. With vibrating throat and open bill it trills on one note sometimes for two or three minutes. When it stops the silence is oppressive. To some it sounds like an angler's reel, to others like the rattle of a distant lawn mower, but never like the insect from which it takes its name. It nests near to water such as marshes or boggy ground but then it will also nest in dry places, such as gorse bushes, both situations where you might hear this retiring rather skulking bird on this walk.

1 Walk south out of the car park, cross Queen's Drive, and wind a little right to continue along the pavement of the busy unclassified road, with St Margaret's Loch beside you on the left. Half way along pause to look up left to see the ruin of St Anthony's chapel and beyond, Arthur's Seat with 'm a t c h s t i c k'

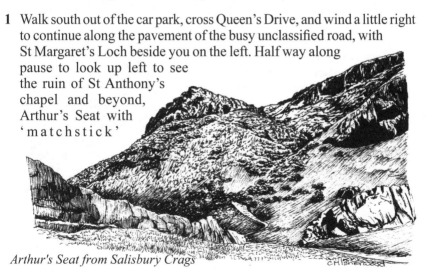

Arthur's Seat from Salisbury Crags

walkers silhouetted against the sky. Then follow a path that leads into trees beside the tranquil water. At the end of the loch, make a small wriggle to pick up a grassy trod that continues parallel with the busy road but well away from it. Press on with fine views of Edinburgh to your right. Soon you can see the Palace of Holyrood, the Parliament buildings, the Castle and Calton Hill. At this point watch out for a wide pebbly track climbing left; this is the track that takes you up below the magnificent Salisbury Crags. It is a long upward ascent where you should pause often to enjoy the ever-increasing views of the lovely city. As you near the top of the track, look for the pretty, diminutive rock rose flowering along the edge of the way. Then gently descend for a short distance to come close to a road.

Walk 11

Rockrose

2 Just before it, turn left onto a cinder path and walk on to where it soon branches, the left branch climbs onto the top of the Crags, the right ascends innumerable steps towards the summit of Arthur's Seat and the middle path, the one you need, leads along the east side of the Crags, with Arthur's Seat towering over you to the right. The sheer slopes of the latter, in spring and summer, are ablaze with golden gorse. The middle path, easy to walk and almost straight, continues well up the grassy slope, above Hunter's Bog, with a large pool in its middle. This is where you may hear a grasshopper warbler. Follow

Grasshopper warbler

42

the path as it bears a little left, and then at the next junction walk right along a red gravel path. Carry on with the ruined chapel high above and then at a large boulder, follow the path as it winds up right and becomes stepped for a short way.

3 Continue up the steadily climbing path as it curves round and then continues ascending left, with the drop to your left steadily increasing. Enjoy the slopes away to your left covered with more flowering gorse. Eventually the path ends after a tiny bit of scrambling, at a track junction, where you turn right to join an upward path with a chain fence to your right. When this goes off right from the path, carry on up with the chain fence now to your left and then when the fencing ends press on along one of several paths that wind on up. At one place there is a very fine easy rock gully that you can follow almost to the summit. Another little scramble leads to a small level area where you again scramble left to the trig point or right to the toposcope. The views are spectacular and extensive over the land and along the Forth – though you might be sharing them with many others who all want to climb Edinburgh's famous hill.

4 Descend the same way or take a zigzagging path down the south-east side of the rock cone to a grassy valley between it and the next hill and then turn left to descend to the 'track junction'. Here ignore your upward path and go on ahead down a wide grassy trod that, towards its lower end, winds left to reach the Queen's Drive and the side of Dunsapie Loch, which lies below high Dunsapie with its ancient fort above. Look for herons and tufted ducks among the gulls and mallards. Walk on down Queen's Drive, using the pavement or a little path beside it. Ignore an early right turn and, after ½ mile/1km, just before the busy road, take the right turn that leads you down steps to arrive at the end of the car park from where you started this superb walk.

Practicals

Type of walk: *Footpaths, wide climbing tracks, cinder paths, stony paths, grassy trods, well pitched paths and a steepish, scrambly climb to the summit, with a similar descent.*

Distance: 5 miles/8km
Time: 4–5 hours
Maps: OS Explorer 350/Landranger 66

Walk 12

Culross

Park in the car park beside the Forth at the west end of the village of Culross, grid ref 983858. Access the village by a signed south turn off the A985.

Make time on your walk to explore the **glorious village of Culross**. During the 1900s people began to realise that it contained many historical buildings and since the 1930s the National Trust for Scotland has been working on their preservation and restoration. The Trust's work has been a wonderful success.

The Town House, Culross

The village is believed to have been founded by Saint Serf during the 6th century. It was he that fostered **St Mungo** after his mother landed in Culross. She had become pregnant before her marriage and because of this her father had her thrown off a cliff. She survived the fall and got into an empty coracle that had drifted towards the shore. The current took her across the Forth to Culross, where she was cared for by St Serf.

Culross during the 16th and 17th century was heavily involved in **coal mining**. In 1575 it was the first place to have a coal mine extending under the sea. It also had a thriving **salt panning industry**. Much of the salt was sent to Holland and the red tiles that make the village such a colourful attractive place were believed to have been brought back in the ships as ballast. The village also made **'girdles'** that is flat iron plates for baking over an open fire.

Walk 12

1 Walk right from the car park, cross the road and go ahead for a few steps. Turn left to pass in front of Culross Palace, which you may wish to visit after your walk. Continue on this curving narrow road, lined with quaint dwellings to climb, left, cobbled Back Causeway between more delectable houses to reach a tiny square with the Mercat Cross in the middle. Press on up where the cobbling stops to reach the ruins of Culross Abbey, another lovely corner. The choir, transepts and tower form the present parish church. Go on with the church away to your right and bear slightly left, at a fork, passing the gable end of a house, with tiny windows, high up. This has caused it to be called 'the House with Evil Eyes'.

2 Immediately, just past the entrance to Park House and Lodge, take a signed footpath, left, along the side of a huge field, with deciduous woodland to your left. Cross a road and press on along a hedged way under mature beech, where you might spot a buzzard being mobbed by a pair of angry crows. Turn right along another path, hedged on both sides with hawthorn, which in May, is heavily laden with blossom and arching over this lovely climbing way, passing through large well kept fields. At its end, wind left, soon to take a path, right, to visit West Kirk, once the original parish church for Culross. The 12th century ruin is very

Crow mobbing buzzard

45

picturesque in its lovely setting, though some of the ancient headstones make for very sad reading.

3 Return to the path and wind on round to a cross of tracks. Here go ahead until you reach an enormous pudding-shaped rock. Keep to its right side and continue ahead on a less distinct path, walking with the fence to your right and a pasture to your left. The way steadily improves as it continues, with forest trees to the right and a hedge to the left. Go through a gate and stroll the footpath as it runs beside the Waas Forest on the right, and telephone lines to your left, along the field margin. Watch out for a stile in the fence into the forest and beyond, walk a narrow path through the magnificent pines. This leads to a little clearing and a fenced grave of a row of stones edged with ferns.

4 Pause beside this little grave. Here James Bald, a girdlesmith, buried his three children, Robert, Agnes and Jeanne, who died of plague on September 14th 1645 at Culross. There is a faint engraving on the headstone. Return to the stile and turn right beyond to continue on the glorious way. Go through a kissing gate and stroll on until you reach a wide track, lined with sycamores, where you turn left. Go past farm buildings, ignore a right turn to a byre and fork right almost immediately at a Y-junction. Beyond continue on through a wide belt of deciduous woodland.

5 As you approach a building among trees (Blair Castle), turn left, and in a short distance turn left again to descend the long access road to the castle. The tarmacked way is lined with rhododendrons and eventually arrives at the unclassified road running parallel with the Forth. Cross the road, walk ahead to go through a gate to a metalled cycle track and turn left. To your right between the track and the Firth is a single-track railway line, very rusty. Stride the track, past reed beds to the left and a pleasing view across the water. Stroll on for 50yds/46m to reach the car park.

Practicals

Type of walk: *A splendid walk through an historic village and then over fine countryside on good paths and tracks. Some might be muddy after rain.*

Distance: 3½ miles/5.5km
Time: 2–3 hours
Maps: OS Explorer 367/Landranger 65

Walk 13

The Fife Coastal Path

Park in Battery Road car park, North Queensferry, directly below the Forth Rail Bridge, grid ref 132808, where there is an orientation panel and signs for the start of the Fife Coastal Path.

The Fife Coastal Path is approximately 89miles/135Km long and is well waymarked. It is divided into sections and each section goes from one town to the next. In each of these towns there is a designated coastal path car park where there is an orientation panel. Car parks have bus stops for those who wish to walk one way and return by public transport. Railway stations on the route all have signs directing you to where the path starts. Although this path starts close to Edinburgh and ends close to busy Dundee, much of the route is through wild spectacular natural landscapes, with some wonderful sands on which to dawdle.

One of most spectacular man-made landmarks in Scotland is the **Forth Rail Bridge**, 1¾ miles/2.7km long and standing 330ft/109m above high tide. This solid cantilever bridge was opened in 1890 and when completed was the longest span in the world. Even today it is believed to be the second longest span of its kind. It took seven years to build by a labour force of 5,000. They used 54,160 tons of steel and 21,000 tons of cement and 6½ million rivets. On a hot summer's day the bridge can expand nearly 10ft/3m.

The Forth Railway Bridge

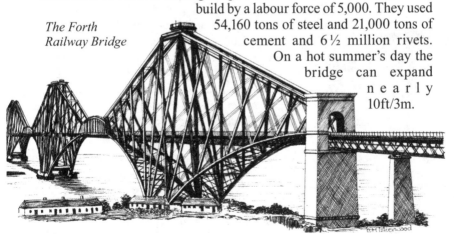

47

1 Follow the signpost directions from the Battery Road car park, or from the railway station, below the Forth Rail Bridge, to the southern start of the coastal path in front of the 1816 Waterloo Well monument, constructed in the shape of Napoleon's hat, North Queensferry. As you climb the paved way look for the coastal path logos set into the wall, on the left, just before you pass below the rail bridge.

Walk 13

2 Go on up the old road to the disused quarries of Carlingnose, now a wildlife reserve and a lovely quiet area. Pause here to watch the fulmars fly into their nests on the many ledges of rock. Take care as you move to the edge of the cliffs, Carlingnose Point, to enjoy the wonderful views up the Forth. The cliffs attract kestrels but they don't nest here, preferring the Forth Bridge where huge flocks of pigeons nest; these provide easy meals for raptors. Here you might find bloody cranesbill and dropwort. Look for islands out in the estuary. In earlier times they had fortresses built on them and then later, during plague times, they were used as places of quarantine. Three hundred million years ago they were volcanoes. As the islands have no predators on them they support large numbers of nesting birds.

3 Descend the path to join a narrow road and follow it until you can wind round to a small beach, Port Laing, where you will want to linger. Then

Bloody cranesbill and dropwort

48

return to the little road. From here you may wish to return by road or by the same route climbing up on the headland to enjoy all those views you missed on the way out. There is another choice too – to continue on the waymarked coastal path, say to Inverkeithing, and make use of public transport for your return.

Fulmars

Practicals

Type of walk: *Rather an up-and-down walk and easy in between. There is always something interesting to see. In winter many wading birds are attracted to the waters and in spring and summer the paths are lined with a wealth of flowers.*

Distance: 2 miles/3.4km
Time: 1–2 hours
Maps: OS Explorer 350/Landranger 65

Walk 14

Aberdour, The Heughs and Humbie Wood

Park just below the railway station at Aberdour in the signed 'village free car park', grid ref 192854. Access Aberdour village via the A921.

Aberdour Castle was built as a hall house around the 1200s. In 1342 the Douglas family became owners of the property and have remained so ever since. The castle was badly damaged in the late 17th century by fire and, after that much of what was left collapsed. In 1725 the family moved to Aberdour House and the surviving east range was used as a barracks and later a school. In 1924 it was placed in state care.

The large and handsome **shelduck** is a bird of tidal flats, sands, dunes and mud. Inland, such as sand hills and links, it haunts shallow pools hunting for land molluscs and other animals. The general plumage of the adult bird is white and black with a rich chestnut band below its neck and a metallic green head.

Aberdour Castle

50

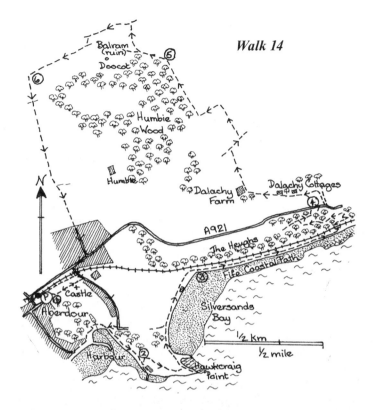

Walk 14

1 Leave the end of the car park, as directed by a large brown sign for
Aberdour Castle and Gardens. Descend wooden steps to a track below.
Walk left to pass the dramatic castle on your right and pass through
the gate ahead into the splendid walled garden, where you asked to
'keep off the grass'. Leave this lovely corner by the gate and walk on
down the road, right, to pass the primary school and on until it ends at
a track. Wind round right, descending more steps at the edge of a little
meadow, with trees all around. This brings you to Aberdour's attractive harbour and to the start of your walk west along the safety-railed
Fife Coastal Path. Look across the Firth to see the Forth rail bridge and
nearer St Colm's Abbey on the island of Inchcolm. '

2 Just before you reach two dwellings very close to the sea, turn left for
a few steps up a cement access road and then right to climb a flight of
arrowed stone steps onto the rough pasture of cliffs. Stroll on the good
path that eventually descends past a light, for yachts, to reach a small
car park. A little path leads out from here to another light on a small
promontory. Go past the 'Boathouse' and walk on to Silversands Bay

with its fine pale curving beach. Carry on past the attractive restaurant, café and toilet section noticing its fine roof. Then bear right along the cinder Coastal Path, with the Firth to your right and the unobtrusive railway hidden among dense forest trees above left.

3 Walk on the pleasing path, fenced and walled for much of the way. Pass under a bridge beneath the railway and carry on with high walls on either side until you reach a signpost at the foot of steps. Look across the Firth from here to see Arthur's Seat, the Salisbury Crags, and the dramatic line of the Pentland Hills. This is the point where you leave the Coastal Path and climb the steps up The Heughs, a glorious steeply sloping area of magnificent forest trees, with a lush understorey where you might find many flowers of the wild strawberry. The steps are steep but easy to climb and when they end a narrow earth path slants away left, climbing steadily through the rampant vegetation. Eventually you reach another signpost. Here go on right up a short, narrower path to reach the A921.

4 Walk right, with much care, along the edge of the road, facing on-coming traffic, for 50yds/46m. Cross when you can see a grassy edge that you can walk on in safety. Turn left up a rough road – the left of two. Climb steadily to go past two bungalows and then a cottage, Carry on up with magnificent views across the Firth. At Dalachy Farm, bear right and pass between the outbuildings. Walk the walled way and then bend right at a T-junction. Take the next left turn from where you can see again the rail bridge across the Forth. Follow the track as it turns right through a gate and begins its descent beside Humbie Wood, with glorious rolling pastures, many covered in gorse, to your right.

5 Follow the track as it winds left around the bottom of the fine deciduous woodland, where you might spot shelduck by a little pond, and press on to another gate. Do not go through but ascend the track that climbs quite steeply to a gate. Beyond, go left and follow the track gently downhill to pass through the gate ahead, then turn left to descend to pass a ruined farmhouse, where you pick up a once reinforced track from the old farm. Bear right along it as it passes through gorse on either side. It then winds left a little and continues down a similar path. Unfortunately it is becoming overgrown and as soon as you can, leave the gorse, left, into pastureland and head on over a rather rough way to a fence.

6 Wind left, go through a gate and walk ahead along a path through burgeoning vegetation, hedged on both sides. This is idyllic but may become difficult later in the year. Cross a track and carry on to the next

track, which you also cross. Beyond, the way becomes a wide track with grass down the middle. Stroll the easier way until you reach the outskirts of Aberdour. Continue down the road ahead until you reach a T-junction. Turn right and take the second left, Hawkcraig Road. Cross the railway bridge and immediately turn right into the lovely gardens of Aberdour Castle. Carry on to the right of the castle to reach the steps up to the car park.

Black-headed gulls in
Silversands Bay

Practicals

Type of walk: *A wonderful ramble of contrasts all on paths and farm tracks except for 50yds/46m of road. The path through the wood and the farm tracks could become muddy after rain.*

Distance: 5miles/8km
Time: 3–4 hours
Maps: OS Explorer 367/Landranger 66

Walk 15

Loch Ore and Harran Hill Wood

Park in the car park, close to the Park Centre, Lochore Meadows Country Park, Crosshill, grid ref 172962. Access this after you have turned off, west, from the B920. The latter is reached from the A92, then north on the B9149 and at the 2nd roundabout leave left to reach the B920 and turn north.

Lochore Meadows includes a vast area of lovely varied countryside. On this walk you pass through woodlands, over grasslands, through meadows and a nature reserve, past ponds and of course round Loch Ore itself. Once the area you walk over was a large coal mining area. It is a wonderful example of land reclamation; over a million trees have been planted.

Mary Pit, walked over early on your walk, was opened in 1904. It produced very high quality coal. The work in the pit was hard, dirty,

Loch Ore

sometimes dangerous and occasionally fatal. Whole families worked at the pit; the men dug the coal, the women and children worked on the surface carrying the coal away from the pithead. It was closed in 1967.

1 From the parking area walk towards the huge reinforced concrete winding gear and the railway engine (pug) and then, where the track divides, take the right branch, to walk through Mary Pit Wood. To your right is the golf course where once much of the Mary Pit was situated. Look out for a grassy left turn through the trees to reach a stile onto the old Pit Road and cross to another stile opposite. If you miss the left turn and, at the track end, reach the Pit Road, further along, take the stile into the field (not the track through the wood). From either stile climb up the pasture towards several sturdy forest trees and here wind left with an old wall to your left, all that remains of Lochore House. Head on to a gate beneath a huge sycamore and pass through the gate beside it.

2 Wind left on a dirt track, known as The Avenue, with a strip of woodland to the right from where come the songs of migrant birds in April. This leads into glorious woodland, known as Ladath Stripe, where wood anemones and celandines, in spring, carpet the ground. Look down through the trees on the left for a glimpse of Loch Ore. Enjoy this lovely path as it moves into mature woodland overlooked by the steep sided Kildownies Wood. Just before the end of the trees on the left, take a left turn to go through a gate into the fine Harran Hill Wood. Climb a little slope and at a T-junction, ignore the waymark and turn right. Follow the good track as it begins its steady descent, steepish in

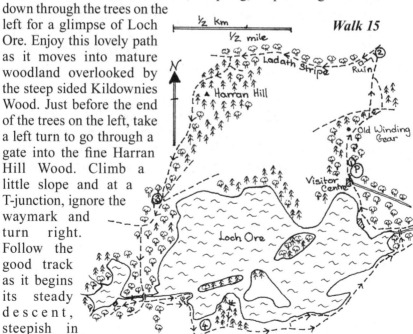

Walk 15

55

parts, through the fine forest trees, keeping parallel with, but often quite a way from, the fenced pasture on the right. Look for bell pits as you descend; these are large grassy hollows from where coal was obtained. Once you near the valley the way eases. Here take a track winding left. It soon joins a forest road, where you descend for a short way to reach a gate onto the old Pit Road once more.

3 Turn right and walk through more delightful woodland. Just before you reach open fields, look for a left turn, which takes you into the Lochore Nature Reserve. In spring the ditch to your right is bordered with large clumps of golden kingcups. Follow the pleasing track to cross a footbridge over the overflow stream from Loch Ore into a smaller loch to your right. Walk on a few steps and turn right soon to reach a bird hide on your right. From here you might see tufted duck, gadwall, dabchick, coot, swan, shelduck and heron. Enjoy this lovely scene. Then return along the track and go ahead over the cross of tracks to continue on around the south side of the extensive Loch Ore. There is a reinforced path all the way and some easy gates to pass through. As you go visit the little viewpoint, on the left, to look across the water to Whaup Island and Moss Island.

Gadwall

4 Continue on perhaps taking a small signposted diversion along the shore side. The path is stony in parts and narrow but easy to walk and brings you out onto the main track once more. Press on to cross the bridge over the River Ore and turn left to walk the track to pass the Outdoor Education Centre. Carry on to join the road and walk left to the Park Centre where there is a restaurant, ranger centre and toilets. Go on ahead to where you have parked.

Practicals

Type of walk: *A pleasing walk through pastures, woodland and beside a large loch.*

Distance: 5 miles/8km
Time: 3 hours
Maps: OS Explorer 367/Landranger 58

Walk 16

Loch Glow and Dummiefarline

Park in a small parking area just before the barrier across the start of the forest track, grid ref 100955. To access this, take the B9097, west from junction 5 on the M90, and leave it just under three miles by a narrow road, west to Cleish and immediately turn left on a narrower road. Continue for three more miles to the forestry track, signed to Loch Glow, on the right.

Delightful **Loch Glow**, in the Cleish Hills, lies six miles from the centre of Dunfermline. It is partly surrounded by plantation forestry. It is a favourite fishing loch for anglers hoping to catch pike, perch and good brown trout. It is also stocked with rainbow trout once a week.

The **Cleish Hills** are low craggy volcanic peaks, dotted with small lochans. The highest is Dumglow (1240ft/379m). On the hill, Dummiefarline (1078ft/330m), look for traces of an ancient hill fort. From the little summit there is a superb view of the surrounding countryside, which must have provided a good outlook for our ancestors worried about attack. Innean means 'anvil' in Gaelic and is often applied to steep-sided volcanic outcrops.

Dummiefarline

1 Walk on along the forest track with tall conifers on either side and continue where it goes right at a junction before emerging from the trees to reach the anglers' (only) parking area on the shore of pleasing Loch Glow. From here there are fine views over the water to various Cleish Hills. Carry on below the dam and go over the footbridge across the overflow, The Lead. Wind on round a short way with the loch, fenced to your left, with fine views ahead of Dumglow's grassy summit,

rising above its skirt of dense forest trees. Follow the path up to take the red metal stile over the fence and begin to strike up the first of the three Inneans, fine grassy hillocks, all part of the Cleish Hills. The narrow grassy path climbs steadily, slightly left, and coming fairly close to the edge of a steepish grassy slope down to the loch shore. Look right to see Dow Loch, a brilliant blue pool in bright sunlight.

2 Follow the path steeply to the top of the ridge and then bear a little left and descend right by the easiest way to the foot of the slope into a secluded steep-sided valley. Stroll right along the foot of the hill and then cross the narrow valley floor, choosing the driest way after heavy rain. Here pick up a narrow path running below the foot of the middle Innean, with glimpses of Lurg Loch ahead, a superb pool. The path curves round left, or you may wish to climb over the hill and join the lower path further on. Stroll on towards Dummiefarline, seen over the top of two lower hillocks, on the indistinct narrow path, dodging round any boggy patches and rounding the corner of a wood, then descend to another small valley, rather muddied by horse riders.

3 Climb up more grassy slopes and wind left, with fine views now of Loch Leven and its islands (see walk 25). Then follow another narrow path that climbs up the easy way to the top of Dummiefarline, winding round low rocks to its pleasing summit and small cairn. The views are superb and here you will wish to linger. Then descend by the same path and continue on a grassy trod towards Lurg Loch passing through a low wall. Or you may wish to walk along the low ridge above to your left. To your right the pretty little loch has a shore of heather, reeds and waterlilies. Follow the path to a gate. Here in spite of cobbling it is very muddy after rain, but use convenient stones to keep dry-footed.

4 Beyond the gate go ahead, bearing slightly right, keeping to a wide grassy swathe. Soon you can spot the narrow road, but between you and it is a very boggy area. Keep to the left of a wooden corral for horses and cross with care to a tied gate. This is easy to undo but do remember to re-tie it securely. Turn right to walk the quiet lane between pastures and then through forest to where you have parked.

Pied wagtail

Practicals

Type of walk: *Short and very pleasant.*

Distance: 3 miles/5 km.
Time: 2 hours
Maps: OS Explorer 367/Landranger 58

Walk 17

Clackmannan and its Tower

Park in Clackmannan's Main Street opposite the Cooperative shop, grid ref 913919.

Clackmannan, often known as "Clacks', stands on a hill a mile from the River Forth. It has one long street of shops, known as Main Street at its lower end, which becomes High Street as it passes the Parish Church. This in turn becomes a grassy trod on the rising spine of a hill where stands the ruined medieval castle, Clackmannan Tower.

Clackmannan is named after the ancient stone associated with the pre-Christian deity Mannan or Mannau. The stone now rests on a larger stone beside the Tolbooth and the Mercat Cross at the end of the Main Street.

The ruins of the Tower stand on the summit of **King's Seat Hill**, in open fields. David II built it in the 1300s. It was sold to Robert Bruce, a relative, in 1359. Part of it collapsed in 1955 because of subsidence caused by coal mining. Historic Scotland has since repaired the damage.

1 Walk west along the street to see the Tolbooth, the extraordinary Stone of Mannan and the Mercat Cross. Walk on up High Street, passing the Church on the left. The road ends at a signposted stile to the right of the gate to Zetland House. Go through the next gate and walk the access track to Clackmannan Tower, on

The Tolbooth, Mercat Cross ans Stone of Mannan

60

King's Seat Hill, and where there is a splendid row of lime trees.

2 Walk on to the left of the tower and through the next kissing gate to enjoy fine views of the Firth of Forth to your left and the Ochils to your right. Walk ahead along the top of the hill through lush grass to look down on Alloa. Then descend gently a fine sloping pasture, where you might spot a hare, with scattered trees about it and a row of lofty beech to your right. Go through a 'gappy' hedge and slant half left and descend to the left corner of another rough hedge. Here locate a stile beside a silvery metal gate (not the red one) and walk right along a good path, just above a large arable field. Follow the path as it curves round right and reaches a stile into mixed woodland.

Walk 17

3 Just beyond stand on the banking on the left to look down on the Black Devon River below on its way to join the River Forth. Stride on the lovely way with wood sorrel, in spring, brightening the forest floor, and continue to the end of the woodland. Walk ahead to join the B910 and go right. Take the next right turn, signposted to the Tolbooth, and walk up to Main Street and turn left to return to your vehicle.

Brown hare

Practicals

Type of walk: *Short and delightful. Good paths and tracks. Some road walking.*

Distance: 1½ miles/2.5km
Time: 1 hour
Maps: OS Explorer 366/Landranger 58

Walk 18

Gartmorn Dam Country Park, Sauchie

From the north take the A908 from Tillicoultry to Sauchie and then follow the sign for the Park, left/east, for 3 ½ miles, to park at the Visitor Centre, grid ref 911941. Park gates open at 8.30am until dusk every day. Free parking.

Gartmorn Dam lies in the centre of the local 370 acre Country Park and Nature Reserve. The area has a rich coal mining history and the reservoir was engineered by Sir John Erskine, 6th Earl of Mar, to provide power for the pumps that drained his Sauchie mines. The reservoir was constructed in 1713 and is the oldest in Scotland.

Great Crested Grebes were once persecuted for their satin breasts – 'grebe fur'. In summer the tippet is rich chestnut, shading to deep brown. The 'Tippet Grebes' as they were once named are noisy birds during the pairing season. They start to court in January, when two birds approach with necks stretched along the water, then rear

Gartmorn Dam

themselves up, breast to breast, stretching necks and spreading wide their 'frills', whilst they fence with their bills. Then one will dive for some weed and dangle it in front of the other, suggesting nest construction. The nest is a floating mass of decaying vegetation moored among reeds.

1 Walk back from the Visitor Centre and turn sharp right to pass through a larger car park. Go through the gate at the end and begin your walk round 'the dam' as it is known locally. Carry on ignoring any left turn. Look out over the lovely stretch of water to see great crested grebe and tufted duck. Continue past small remnants of buildings once part of Sheriffyards Colliery, now almost lost under the rich vegetation and well hidden by trees. You might spot huge mounds of mine waste supporting sturdy forest trees and perhaps a seat from where you have a good view over the loch. Follow the track ahead stepping on small bits of old sleepers and noting the straightness of the way reminding you that this was once part of the old mineral line that linked Alloa Port on the Firth of Forth with the colliery. Then the track moves a little away from the loch and you have glimpses of the water through woodland. Eventually the track carries on beyond the end of the reservoir and passes through pleasing deciduous woodland, the site of the major part of the Sheriffyards Colliery.

2 At the T- junction turn right to walk a similar track, hedged, and then with pasture land to the left and arable to the right. Go past a house named Sheriffyards and press on along the pleasing way to cross a footbridge over a stream. Turn right immediately to continue on round 'the dam' where, in a little bay, more great crested grebes court and tufted ducks

Tufted duck

Walk 18

63

idle in the sun. Carry on past two artificial hills clad in young trees, both old mining sites. Stroll on the pleasing way where in spring the trees are full of migrant birds advertising their presence in order to attract a mate and the woodland floor is carpeted with wood sorrel and celandines.

3 At the actual dam, turn right and walk a wider way and from where you have a fine view up the whole length of the loch. Go past the sunken garden on the left, once filter beds, and wind round left to the Visitor Centre, where many swans congregate.

Teal

Practicals

Type of walk: *Flat tracks, well waymarked and easy to walk.*

Distance:	3 miles/5 km
Time:	2 hours
Maps:	OS Explorer 366/Landranger 58

Walk 19

Lewis Hill

Park in a layby on either side of the road, grid ref 758878. Access this by the M9 and leave it at the 'Stirling Services' roundabout to take the A872, north, signed to Bannockburn. Turn left almost immediately, then left again at a T-junction to cross over the motorway. Go ahead at a crossroads and right at next two Y-junctions, following the occasional sign for the North Third Trout Fishery. The parking laybys lie less than a mile beyond. If full, there are more laybys before you reach the most useful one.

The view from the summit of **Lewis Hill** is stunning. Look on the skyline for Ben Ledi, Stuc a' Chroin, Ben Vorlich, Ben Chonzie, the Ochils, the Lomonds and the Pentland Hills. Below the Craigs, you have fine views down through the great rocks and the trees to the reservoir, North Third, which was constructed in 1931. At that time a Bronze Age battle-axe was discovered and is now housed in Edinburgh's Royal Museum of Scotland.

The reservoir is the haunt of several hundred **Grey Lag and Canada Geese**, who spend much time on the grassy side of the reservoir. They are diurnal feeders, cropping grass, clover, or seeking out grain. They sleep in open country or beside quiet water. Look for them flying in ordered lines or in chevron formations. If you walk this way in May or June you will enjoy watching the geese and their

Sauchie Craigs, Lewis Hill

65

goslings lingering on the grassy bank of the reservoir or sailing over the water.

1 From the north side of the road climb the banking and then walk the unsigned but distinct path into the forest, where you are likely to see bullfinch, spotted flycatcher and chaffinch. At a division of the way take the right branch and stroll on. The trees lie well back from the path and the extra light and sunshine encourages a fine array of wild flowers. Continue on the path as it now climbs quite steeply to an open area from where you can see the Forth in the distance. The trees are scattered here. Then the path steepens again, but is still fairly easy to ascend to another high open area where the forest lies to your right and you have good views of the surrounding hills to the left.

½ km
½ mile
North Third Reservoir
Windy Yet
Fort
Lewis Hill 261m.
Craigs Wood

Walk 19

2 A little more gentle climbing and you have your first real view of the loch. Continue on the narrow, delightful, almost level path through heather and broom. Take care as you move nearer to the edge to look down on the huge boulders and then the conifers below. Descend a little and then ascend a rocky slope up Lewis Hill and in a few more steps you reach the white painted trig point where you will want to pause.

Spotted flycatcher

3 Go on gently descending above Sauchie Craig and into woodland. Where the path seems to divide take the upper path. Both soon join. Then pass, to your left, two rounded hillocks covered in lush grass, believed to be the site of an ancient fort. Pass below ancient oaks as the way winds round left and goes on down. It edges the hillocks seen earlier. To the right the land drops very steeply to a valley, Windy

Yet Glen. Bracken covers the slope down and reduces the feeling of exposure.

4 Follow the path as it winds sharp right and carries on in zigzags down the steep slope just viewed. Take care here; it is a good track but intermittently the natural rock steps are steep. Finally the way eases and winds right and then it goes left down to the floor of the attractive glen. Turn left at the waymark towards the dam of the reservoir. There is one rather miry section but if you step, right, before it and then cross on dead branches you keep dryshod. Carry on to a waymark by a fence. Here climb the fence to join a good path on the other side.

5 Dawdle on the signed way with the fence to your right, to the dam, which you cross. Carry on over a grassy area and then cross another dammed area. Walk the overflow bridge above the Bannock Burn and then wind left at the far end. The path beyond leads to the top of a short flight of steps, left, easily missed when the grass is lush. After descending, head on along a stretch of duckboarding then up a little slope into a willow copse on more duckboarding. From this side of the reservoir you have a dramatic view of the Craigs. Cross a small stream entering an alder copse, where monkeymusk flowers together with forget-me-nots.

6 Carry on to cross Kings Yet Burn on a long bridge and bear round with the path, past a hut for anglers. Beyond, the path is reinforced as it passes the end of the lovely sheet of water. Follow it as it winds away right, with Bannock Burn flowing into the reservoir to your left and forestry beyond. Ignore the first bridge and walk on across a field with clear-fell to your right to reach a footbridge and the narrow lane where you have parked. Turn left to rejoin your vehicle.

Practicals

Type of walk: *A joy. The paths are good and never in any doubt. The views are spectacular. The bird life and wild flowers are a delight.*

Distance: 3 miles/5km

Time: 2 hours

Maps: OS Explorer 366/Landranger 57

Walk 20

Bridge of Allan to Dunblane

Park on the bridge in Bridge of Allan, grid ref 789976. If the spaces here are full there is roadside parking all through the town except on the main street, Henderson Street, and a large public car park beside the co-op, grid ref 792974.

Bridge of Allan lies on the Allan Water, a tributary of the River Forth. Around the 1550s quantities of **gold, silver and copper** were extracted from the woods above the few cottages, which were constructed at either end of the bridge, built in 1520, to replace the old ford across the River Allan. The town later, in Victorian times, became a spa town.

Splendid **Dunblane Cathedral** was once the seat of the bishops of Dunblane. Today the building is owned by the Crown and is looked after by Historic Scotland. Find time to visit this lovely church to see its glorious exterior and interior. Notice the bell tower once free-standing. It was incorporated into the building in the 13th century. It was heightened in the 15th century – look for the

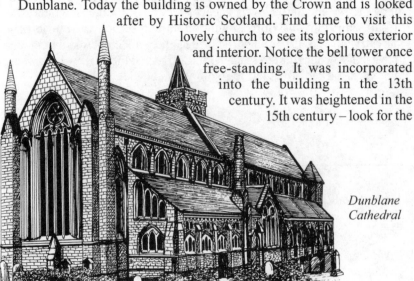

Dunblane Cathedral

change in the colour of the stone work and the change in style of the windows.

1 Take the road beside the Water of Allan, Blairforkie Drive, and follow it for 330yds/300m to a footpath, signed on the left, for the Darn Road to Dunblane. Follow behind houses and then beside fields to keep along above the river. Soon climb a bank from where there are fine views, left, to the Water, full of rapids and little falls. Keep left at a junction to descend steps through a steep-sided gully. Cross a bridge over a tributary burn at the bottom, and climb the far side into open beech woods, with celandines and blue-bells in spring. Continue high above the river until the path goes down a fenced way to pass a cave, thought to have been the model for Ben Gunn's cave in Robert Louis Stevenson's Treasure Island. Beyond, ignore the bridge over the river unless you wish to picnic on the fine sandy area downstream from the bridge on the far side. Look for dippers and grey wagtails by the water here.

Walk 20

2 Carry on along the path with the river to your left, then cross an open grassy space to reach a signposted path. Turn left, cross a wooden bridge over the Wharry Burn and continue up a walled path through woodland, which becomes sunken through fields. Keep on the path that runs along the lower edge of Dunblane Golf Course watching out for stray golf balls. It emerges onto the B8033.

3 Cross the busy road and walk left to take the first turn right into the town. Walk up the delightful main street to the cathedral at the top, which you may want to visit. Then carry on round the cathedral to follow the road uphill. At a gap between two houses, look for a signed path into Holme Hill woods, and walk up the lovely beech-lined way. Bear left at the top and then wind right to come out between gate-posts onto the B8033 again. Turn right past the entrance to Dunblane

Hydro and then immediately go left up a narrow lane called Newton Loan. Climb this between high walls with trees to the left until it exits into a housing estate. Go right to the T-junction and turn left. About 660ft/200m along, turn right into another road, then almost immediately take a track on the right signed to Dykedale and Sherriffmuir. After 330ft/100m turn right into Dykedale Wood following a path to Kippenrait. The path can be wet in places. It comes out at a small car park onto the Sherriffmuir Road. Turn right and walk downhill to the junction where you turn left.

4 This narrow road is the Glen road which although surfaced is closed to traffic and continues through pleasant woodland. The road crosses a high bridge over the Wharry Burn and follows a ledge along the side of the steep valley, the Kippenrait Glen. This is a delightful part of the walk. In places the road has fallen away, but these bits are fenced. Eventually the road leaves the glen. Keep left at a junction, ignore a footpath sign on the right, and go left at the next junction. At the fork ahead turn right and follow the road down through large houses and woodland to a left bend. Take a path on the right, which runs down beside a grassy area then bears left along the top of a steep river terrace. Take the right branch at a fork and come down the fenced and stepped way to rejoin Blairforkie Drive just at the end of the bridge.

Grey wagtail

Practicals

Type of walk: *Delightful, interesting easy walk with some road walking.*

Distance: 5½ miles/9km
Time: 2–3 hours
Maps: OS Explorer 366/Landranger 57

Walk 21

Dumyat

Park in the car park to the north of the A91, at Blairlogie, grid ref 831968. On the Explorer map it is marked on the other, wrong, side of the road.

Dumyat, pronounced Dum-i-at, is a hill at the western extremity of the Ochil Hills. It is a volcanic plug and is a distinct and very craggy hill unlike the other rolling grassy Ochils. At the top is a memorial to the **Argyll and Sutherland Highlanders**, a trig point and a cairn with a beacon on the top. The latter was commissioned for the Queen's Jubilee, 1977. It was carried up and erected on Dumyat by a Scout group and was lit as one of a chain of beacons as part of the Jubilee celebrations.

Look for **wheatears** on this walk. A wheatear can be recognised by its white rump. Its name is derived from this and has nothing to do with wheat. It is constantly on the move, flitting from stone to stone, tuft to tuft repeating its 'chack, chack' call. Its usual nesting places on the hills are stone walls, clefts in rocks and rabbit holes.

Beacon and cairns, Dumyat

1 Walk out of the back of the car park, up steps and over a stile onto a path where you turn left. As you approach a cottage take a small path on the right, very steep in places, which climbs up outside the garden fence. Descend to a burn and step across, then continue up the far bank. The path winds away from the burn up onto a grassy promontory, then goes to the right through gorse bushes and climbs up along the side of the deepening ravine. Chiffchaffs call from all the bushes in spring. Gradually the slope eases and the path moves away from the edge into a shallow bowl. Follow a tributary burn left, then step across and carry on along the clear path as it contours round a spur and runs down to another burn. Cross this too and then turn left on a less clear path, which winds its way up a rather boggy valley (do not be tempted to keep on the clearer path which climbs the steep hillside opposite unless you have a good head for heights). Negotiate the fence crossing at a gate, then follow an earth bank up the steepening head of the valley to join a broad path like a motorway which is the more usual way up Dumyat. Turn right.

2 This path is very easy to follow as it rises to a col, drops to ford a burn and rises again through a shallow valley. At the highest point on the next col look for a small, distinct path going right and take this across a raise. Step over a fence, notice a path coming in on the left, and carry on to the top of Castle Law, which at 1223ft/374m is the second highest summit on Dumyat. There are two cairns and suggestions of the remains of a fort, and

½ km
½ mile
N
Menstrie Glen
Walk 21
Dumyat 419m.
Castle Law
Dumyat Farm
Blairlogie
A91

Wheatear

a superb view over the Forth Plain and of the highest top of Dumyat. Wheatears flit about the moorland flashing their white rumps, skylarks sing and meadow pipits parachute in spring.

3 Return along the same path but fork right at the junction and go down into a dip. Cross a bog then walk round the end of the fence and rejoin the main path. Turn right to continue to the rocky summit of Dumyat, which is crowned with a cairn with a beacon basket, a trig point, a memorial and two plaques. Enjoy the superb view. The abrupt slope along the south side of the Ochils is very obvious and dramatic.

4 To descend, follow a small path leading away from the cairn round the north-eastern side of the summit ridge, gradually descending. It crosses a depression and two paths leave it here on the right. Probably either will do, but the second is more obvious so take that one, heading towards the dam of Lossburn Reservoir. Go down the valley, zigzagging in steeper places, and cross the boggy moorland below. Look for red grouse and listen for curlews bubbling.

5 Join a track at a three way junction and turn right, to walk down the edge of the moor above the Menstrie Burn in its deep glen. Carry on round the corner, enjoying the unfolding view of the Forth Plain. Walk above the waterworks and go down steeply on the very rough track for a few yards to sheep pens. Then go on the now level track past two houses and above a wood. Where the track begins to go downhill into the wood take a small path on the right. Cross a burn on a sleeper footbridge and contour the delightful grassy hillside above the trees, with the crags of Dumyat towering above on your right. The path gradually descends to run along behind the car park. Turn left over the stile and return to your car.

Practicals

Type of walk: *A less well-used route up splendid Dumyat, joining the usual one on the ridge. This one involves more climbing by starting at the hill foot and while the paths are clear, they are not so eroded. The track back down Menstrie Glen is good.*

Distance: 6 miles/9.5km

Time: 4 hours

Maps: OS Explorer 366/Landranger 57 and 58 (part on each)

Walk 22

Ben Cleuch

Park near the top of the road beside the Mill Burn in Tillicoultry, grid ref 914975. To reach this turn north off the A 91 at the west end of the village, just past the entrance to the golf course.

The summit of **Ben Cleuch** at 2363ft /721m, is the highest of the Ochil Hills. This range of rolling hills extends from Stirling in the west to the M90 south of Perth in the east. The hills are mainly volcanic and the steep south escarpment is the result of a fault. Quartz-dolerite was quarried here for road stone, and many minerals have been found and mined including copper, silver and gold.

Waterfall, Mill Glen

The **range of hills** shows a steep front to the villages and towns that lie along its southern foot. These are known as the 'Hillfoot Towns'. They developed here as mill towns, using the water-power from the steep burns. There were eight textile mills in Tillicoultry at one time.

Walk 22

1 Walk to the top of the road and go up steps and through a small park. Follow the path beside the Mill Burn to pass through a gate into a narrow ravine. After a short distance notice a hole in the cliff on the right, called the Lion's Cave. Cross the burn on a small arched bridge, with a gate in the middle, then climb a flight of steps which takes you high above the gorge, on your right, with a steep drop into a quarry on your left. The path carries on as a ledge along a cliff face, fenced on the other side. Beyond another gate, continue to cross the next bridge over the burn. Climb a flight of steps and then go on to cross two more bridges. Ascend again to follow a concrete pathway by the burn to take another bridge and climb steps to reach a junction. Turn right up more steps, then along and down. Look below for the remnants of an old dam left from the days when water powered the mills. The path then comes down to the burn again, crosses another bridge and climbs steps at the far side. Admire the fine waterfall where the Dairglen Burn joins the Gannel Burn to form the Mill Burn. Turn right.

2 This path is not fenced and is quite exposed in places, so children should be kept under close control. It is a delightful narrow contouring path making its way round the steep hillside above the Mill Burn, coming out to the mouth of the glen quite high on the hillside and giving fine views over Tillicoultry and the whole of the Forth Valley beyond. The slope below eases as the path turns a corner. Do not take

either of the first two paths going steeply up on the left. Wait until you come to the top of a downward flight of wooden steps. Here you can see a seat, up to your left, where you might like to pause before turning to make a start on the steep ascent. At first the path is indistinct and there are several options, although they all rejoin. Then it becomes clear and definite, winding more gently round the side of the hill, once more above the Mill Glen.

3 After ¼ mile/0.5 km the path rises across the open hillside, where you may be serenaded by skylarks. The grass is studded with tormentil and there are scattered harebells. At the remains of an old fence there is a path junction. Keep straight on enjoying the good views along the easier way. Pass a cairn, then a tiny lochan full of cotton grass to descend slightly to a gate. Turn left just before you reach it and wind down into a narrow valley to join a contouring path. Cross the bottom of the valley and climb the far side. The path now leads gently up to the top of Andrew Gannel Hill 2175ft/669m, where it swings left to a craggy point. The views are superb. This is not actually the summit; you have to walk north to a point beside the fence for that. Then follow the good clear path down the far side to the dip between Andrew Gannel Hill and Ben Cleuch. It is a little boggy in the bottom. Climb up the far side to a fence leading out to The Law 2051ft/638m. Step over and join the 'motorway'; this is the way most people climb Ben Cleuch. Follow this broad path, with the fence to your right, to the summit. Here there is a trig point, a view indicator, and a small stone shelter.

4 Leave the top, continuing in the same direction with the fence to your right, on a good clear path that runs steeply downhill to a col. Cross the fence in the bottom and climb gently up to the top of Ben Ever 2040ft/622m. There are two small cairns on top, the left one which is farther from the path seems to be the higher. Then carry on down the far side on a good path. At the foot of the first steep bit cross another path but keep on in the same direction. Cross a rise and come down to a fence junction with a gate. Do not go through the gate, instead cross a stile in the fence on the left just before it. The path keeps on clearly over the next rise and then begins to descend steeply. Where it is very steep it makes zigzags. It works its way down into a hollow below the next rise, and here it joins the end of an old grassy quarry track, which runs down to the left towards Mill Glen. This gives very pleasant walking. It makes a sharp bend to the right and then contours; look out for a large cairn on the left just beyond a small quarry (or borrow pit). This marks the start of another path, which you must take to avoid ending up at

the new quarry. Follow the path as it slants gently downwards across the hillside. Eventually it ends at a fence with a large notice forbidding access as there is a quarry ahead. Turn left and a few steps downhill go left again to slant back in the other direction, still gently downhill. Negotiate a zigzag in the path, which brings you down to the junction at the top of steps on your outward route. Turn right, go down to cross the bridge and retrace your path down Mill Glen, enjoying the views of the waterfalls from the other direction.

Skylark

Practicals

Type of walk: *A most enjoyable climb combining a deep glen full of waterfalls, typical of this side of the Ochils, with open grassy hilltops and fantastic views.*

Distance: 8 miles/13km
Time: 6 hours
Maps: OS Explorer 366/Landranger 58

Walk 23

Dollar Glen

Park in the large car park, part way up the hill, on the right, grid ref 964981. To access this turn north off the A91 in Dollar and drive uphill beside the burn, following signs for Dollar Glen.

Dollar Glen is dominated by the fifteenth century stronghold of the powerful Campbells, Earls of Argyll. It is sometimes called **Castle Gloom** (thought to be derived from Gaelic 'glom' meaning gorge), with the Burn of Care on one side and the Burn of Sorrow on the other. In 1654 the castle was sacked by the Scots in retaliation for the Duke of Argyll's support for Cromwell. The Campbells abandoned the Castle but continued to own the lands. When the earldom was restored in 1661 the family chose to occupy property in Stirling.

Castle Campbell, Dollar Glen

1 Cross the road from the car park and go .through the small gate opposite into lovely woodland. The path winds round to the right along the edge of a steep slope, then descends steps to just above Dollar Burn. Turn left and follow the turbulent water to a walled viewing platform, then carry on down where the steep sides of the ravine are clothed in a luxuriant growth of mosses, ferns, including hard shield fern, golden saxifrage and wild garlic. Emerge onto an open grassy area where two paths join from the left. Cross a bridge over the burn and immediately climb steeply up steps, zigzagging higher up, to reach the top of the wood. Beyond the fence is a golf course. Turn right and walk along the edge of the wood, then into the trees through more tall beech.

Walk 23

¹/₄ Km   ¹/₄ mile

N

Castle Campbell

2 Follow the path, which suddenly reaches an edge of a ravine where Castle Campbell stands poised dramatically ahead on the far side of a deep gorge cut out by the Burn of Sorrow. A short detour to the right leads to an even better view. Then go on down the slope towards the castle. At a gated junction, take the small path to the right, which leads down into the gorge to another viewing platform. The gorge takes a right-angled bend here and is extremely narrow and deep. Look for dippers which frequent the gorge; you may be able to look down on one as it runs under the water.

Dipper

3 Return to the main path and continue down to cross a bridge below the castle. If tired you can climb steps from here and go directly to the castle where there is an excellent tearoom. Otherwise turn left along a narrow path running above the river with primroses and wood sorrel on the bank in spring. Descend a little to cross another bridge and carry on up the far side. Soon you can see that the burn comes down in a series of waterfalls; here the path leaves the main glen and climbs a side valley, zigzagging higher up, then swings right to cross a spur. There is a fence to the right which you should not cross as the spur ends in a cliff. Ignore a path running up the spur to your left; continue along the path by the fence as it drops down slightly to a bridge. Again ignore the path going left. There is a splendid waterfall dropping into a circular pool above the bridge.

4 Cross the bridge and turn right along the path at the far side. Look for dippers again in the burn, and admire the fine waterslides and polished potholes. Then the burn vanishes behind an outcrop of rock. The path descends steeply; where it levels there is a branch to the right which will bring you to a viewing platform for another fine waterfall. Return to the path and go on to a gate beyond which you join another path and bear left, then right, to reach the castle. You may want to tour the castle or just visit the tearoom.

5 Then leave down the metalled road and soon turn right to go down steps and cross the Burn of Care by a bridge. Walk down the far side, then down steps followed by a long stepped walkway. At the bottom take the right fork and go down to another viewing platform at the foot of the amazing narrow gorge you saw earlier from the other end. Return to the main path and climb another stepped walkway. Beyond it the path continues as a wide ledge along the cliff until it descends to the junction where you turned left near the start of the walk. Bear left to climb steps out of the ravine and return along the top to the car park.

Golden saxifrage

Practicals

Type of walk: *Through a spectacular gorge with splendid waterfalls and luxuriant vegetation. The paths are well maintained and fenced where necessary.*

Distance: 2 miles/3.5km
Time: 1 ½– 2hours
Maps: OS Explorer 366/Landranger 58

Walk 24

River Devon and Rumbling Bridge

Park at the south-west end of the village, Pool of Muckhart, on either side of the quiet road leading south off the A91, close to the village hall, grid ref 999006.

The old road to **Muckhart Mill** would have been much used by mill workers to access their work place. The road continued to the Rumbling Bridge, giving access to the east side of the River Devon.

The glorious double bridge, known as the **Rumbling Bridge,** gives its name to the small village. The rumbling noise, which gives the bridge its name, is caused by boulders grinding under the waterfalls. The bridge crosses the gorge 120ft above the river. The lower bridge dates from 1700 and the upper one was constructed in the 1800s.

Rumbling Bridge

81

The **River Devon** rises on Blairdenon Hill in the Ochils. On its way to the Forth it has been dammed, creating several reservoirs. It flows east and then south-east.

It turns south-west at Crook of Devon, then goes on westward across its flood plain along the foot of the Ochils. It reaches the River Forth west of Alloa.

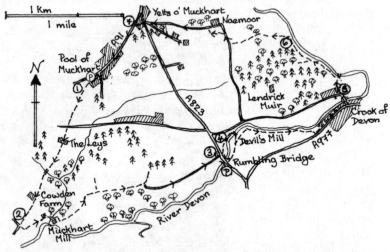

Walk 24

1 From the parking area, walk on along the road to where it ends in a cul de sac. Head on along the signposted reinforced footpath, pleasingly edged with forest trees, to reach a narrow road. Cross and go ahead along the access track to pass through the buildings of The Leys farm. Go through a gate and head across a pasture to another gate then descend steadily, keeping beside a small dry valley to your left, once part of the main route to Pool of Muckart; over time the old road has sunk lower and lower and formed the dry valley. The path then drops to a rough area just before a ford where there is a wooden footbridge if you need it. Beyond, the tree-shadowed track begins to climb gently with pastures to the right and hill slopes to the left and carries on to go through a gate to Cowden farm. The access track beyond is much firmer and makes for easier walking to reach a cross of tracks and narrow roads.

2 Turn left and descend a glorious tree-lined track to reach Muckhart Mill, picturesquely set below the track. It has a fine waterwheel and far down you can spot white water descending to the River Devon below.

Follow the track as it begins to wind uphill, passing a huge limekiln to your right. Go on climbing, passing below many fine beech trees and then out into more open countryside. Head on past Blairhill farm and cottages, ignoring any left turns. Wind round right with the track, now with fine views of the Cleish Hills. The way becomes metalled just before it reaches the A823.

3 Cross with care to reach an iron gate, which is quite difficult to open. Beyond there is an awkward step down to the path. If the gate is locked or the step too difficult, cross the bridge and take the path on the left to walk above the river, but, by taking this path you will miss all the viewing platforms. Once down the awkward step walk on for a few steps to take the railed stepped way to a viewing platform to see the magnificent Rumbling Bridge with its much older bridge beneath. Far down the very deep ravine the Devon hurtles through sheer-sided cliffs and over and around boulders in a white-topped fury. All this is seen through many fine trees.

4 Continue along the path through the glorious wooded slopes of the ravine. Go past a picnic table and on to several viewing platforms to see the raging river in its deep chasm. Then wind right to cross the footbridge, listening for more rumbling, and turn right to climb a long flight of easy steps to the path high above the river. Walk left and enjoy the lovely woodland to descend steps to a more open area to walk beside the fast flowing water. Eventually the river winds away left and the path leads ahead and up steps to the side of the A977. Turn left and walk along the pavement of the busy road to the village of Crook of Devon. Continue along the main street until you can turn left into Naemoor Road to cross the 'weak bridge' over the River Devon just before it makes it dramatic 'crook' turn.

5 Climb the steadily rising road and take, nearly at the end of the village, a signed footpath with a wooden fence on the left and a wall on the right. Continue along the footpath where it moves into the open and has deer fencing on either side overlooked by the Ochils. Stride on to the side of the River Devon after it has made its 'crook' turn. Ignore the footbridge and walk left beside the sweetly flowing river on your right. Stride on beside the hurrying water, the path indistinct in places as it passes beside a plantation on the left. Watch out for a flock of gold-finches that take off from thistle heads along the riverbank. When the plantation ends head towards a gate but do not pass through; instead keep to a fenced path beside the river. Carry on beside the river until the path ends.

6 Turn left, away from the river and walk a raised grassy swathe through a huge pasture, heading towards a well-wooded shelterbelt. Beyond the trees continue on the track, wet in places after heavy rain and at an open gate bear right along a metalled way. Stroll on to reach a sign on the left that directs you along a short footpath to the side of a ditch and walk right beside it. This brings you to a metalled lane where you bear left to stroll through delightful rolling countryside to reach the A823 leading to Yetts o' Muckart. Cross with care and continue along another footpath, which soon winds right to join the A91.

7 Cross and walk left along a raised grassy path that, after a ¼ mile, brings you to Pool of Muckhart, with its church and cemetery tucked away behind trees. Stride on to pass the village coffee shop and also the Inn at Muckhart. Cross the A-road and then bear left to return to the parking area.

Goldfinch

Practicals

Type of walk: *Very pleasing countryside; generally good paths and tracks, some muddy after heavy rain. Dramatic bridge and river gorge.*

Distance: 8 miles/13km
Time: 4–5 hours
Maps: OS Explorer 369/ Landranger 58

Loch Leven National Nature Reserve

Park in the car park in front of Mill Bridge Hall, Kinross, grid ref 119020. Leave by the exit, walk ahead to the main street and turn right to reach the first bus stop on the right side of the road, opposite the defunct town hall. For information on buses to RSPB's Vane Farm Visitor Centre, telephone Traveline Scotland 0871 200 2233.

The Loch Leven Heritage Trail, opened in 2008, is a traffic-free, level, reinforced path, on which you cannot get lost, linking the RSPB's Vane Farm Visitor Centre with Kinross. Sadly, as yet, there is no path between Kinross and Vane Farm, which would complete the loop round the lovely loch. To avoid having to return by the same 8 miles, take the bus from Kinross to Vane Farm.

Loch Leven fills over 13 square km of low ground between the Ochil, Cleish and Lomond hills. The loch is very shallow with over half

The Sluice House, Loch Leven

of it being less than two metres in depth, which is ideal for **up-ending ducks and swans** to obtain small creatures and plants in food-rich water.

In spite of the title of this walk only small parts of the shore are accessible, views of the lake are limited but there are many distant glimpses. Really much of the trail is through **woodland** making it a very pleasant walk.

The loch has seven islands, the largest being St Serf's where there is a ruined priory. **Mary, Queen of Scots**, was imprisoned in Loch Leven castle on Castle Island from the middle of 1567 until she managed to escape in May 1568. Three of the islands were revealed when the level of the loch, during 1830 to 1832, was lowered to control the water supply to nearby mills. At the same time the bed of the River Leven, the loch's only outflow, was realigned and sluice gates installed.

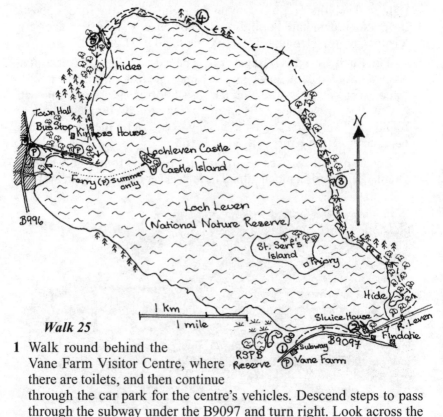

Walk 25

1 Walk round behind the Vane Farm Visitor Centre, where there are toilets, and then continue through the car park for the centre's vehicles. Descend steps to pass through the subway under the B9097 and turn right. Look across the vast loch to the Bishop Hill, part of the Lomond Hills. From the trail

you have a good view of the ruin on St Serf's island. As you walk, in late spring, every bush seems to have its own sedge warbler. Soon you reach a pretty boggy area where grow marsh cinquefoil, marsh lousewort, northern marsh and common spotted orchids, ragged robin and yellow iris.

2 Press on into woodland. Where you emerge from the trees, go through the barrier, on the left, to join the access road to the Sluice House, with five arches through which surges water from the loch to become the River Leven. Walk on, right, a short way along the road and then cross the fine footbridge over the hurrying water. Follow the path to pass through woodland on both sides. Listen as you go for siskin, willow warbler and garden warbler. Turn left to visit a hide overlooking a lochan where you might spot tuftie, shoveller, coot, mallard, teal, swan and heron. Return to the path and carry on through mature pines and silver birch, the haunt of red and grey squirrel.

Marsh cinquefoil

3 Stroll on with a vast field to your right, and woodland to the left, from where you have a glimpse of a huge line of geese and many swans on the loch. The path continues raised above the ground on either side and you have a better view of the loch. The way soon enters more woodland where spotted woodpecker and long tailed tit pass through the branches. The trees are eventually left behind and, to the left, stretches a large area of grass where cattle graze, with no clear view of the loch. Pass through two gates over a farm track and then through fields from where you can see the loch once again. Cross three bridges in turn over a dyke.

Sedge warbler

4 Go with the path, edged with buttercups and white clover, as it winds left and then right nearer to the shore. To your right, look for the tower of a ruined church. Where the trail moves a short way from the shore take a narrow path beside the water, through pines. As you stroll enjoy the little beaches; it is very pleasant to sit on a bench and listen to the gentle lapping water. Pass through an avenue of Scots pine and then

you see more of the loch. Look for the grassy path that continues over a meadow full of wild flowers to walk parallel with the trail. Both join up just before a bridge over the Back Burn, which you cross. Continue on past some fine white willow trees to reach Mary's Gate.

5 Turn left for Kinross and, after a meadow, stroll into conifer woodland and press on. Cross a footbridge to follow the trail between wet meadows. Soon you come beside a magnificent wall and then you can peep through the Fish Gate of Kinross House to see the splendid mansion. Look across the loch, at this point, to the ruin on Castle Island and then dawdle on into Kirkgate Park. Keep along beside the loch, then almost at the end of the path, turn right at a fork and then left on the very narrow walled vehicle access road. Go ahead, cross a road and soon turn left to reach the car park.

Bugle and wild strawberry

Practicals

Type of walk: *Lovely walk but a woodland one rather than a lochside stroll.*

Distance: 8 miles/12.5km
Time: 4 hours
Maps: OS Explorer 369/Landranger 58

Walk 26

West Lomond

Park in the second car park, on the left, of the minor road running along the west side of the Lomond Hills, grid ref 173069. To reach this turn south off the A91 along Station Road in the village of Gateside. After ½ mile/1km, turn right at a T-junction. Note a layby after 110yds/100m which is the Bonnet Stane car park, but it is better to continue along the road for a further 1¼ miles/2 km to the next, larger, car park.

The calciferous sandstone at the base of the Lomond Hills was laid down underwater in layers, which are of differing hardness. Over time they have been eroded by ice, wind and water, and the softer layers have worn away more rapidly than the harder ones, giving rise to caves, tunnels, and extraordinary shapes of which one, the spectacular **Bonnet Stane,** is like an enormous mushroom.

The Bonnet Stane

C. Misherwood

John Knox's Pulpit is a huge outcrop where again the layers have eroded differentially. At the time of the Reformation congregations gathered here in secret and the preacher stood on the jutting rock to address them. Legend has it that an angel with drawn sword stood on top of the rock to protect the minister below.

Again the Covenanters Glen is a craggy outcrop known as the Devil's Burdens. Legend has it that local witch, **Carlin Maggie,** was turned to stone here after she dared challenge Satan on nearby Bishop Hill.

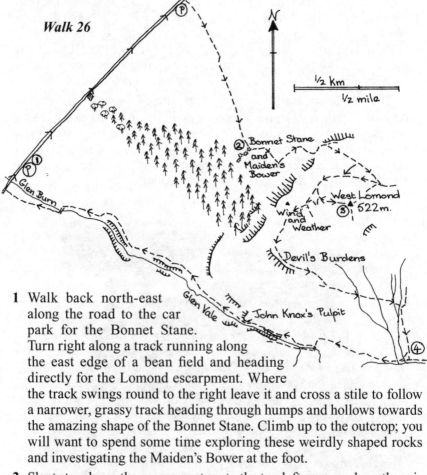

Walk 26

1 Walk back north-east along the road to the car park for the Bonnet Stane. Turn right along a track running along the east edge of a bean field and heading directly for the Lomond escarpment. Where the track swings round to the right leave it and cross a stile to follow a narrower, grassy track heading through humps and hollows towards the amazing shape of the Bonnet Stane. Climb up to the outcrop; you will want to spend some time exploring these weirdly shaped rocks and investigating the Maiden's Bower at the foot.

2 Slant steeply up the grassy pasture to the top left corner where there is a waymark. Cross a derelict wall and climb the steep slope beside the

fence to another waymark. Here the fence and path turn left, running along the slope and so the gradient is easier for a time. Cross a stile and wind round a high dry valley on what was once an old path, still climbing steeply. It leaves the valley to reach a rocky outcrop on a spur. Just beyond this the most obvious way is a sheep path running along the top of crags; do not take this but look for a small grassy trod going up a shallow gully on the right, and follow this up onto the plateau. Head away from the edge, with a steeper slope to your right and the summit cone of West Lomond towering beyond. If you continue along the small path you will meet the 'motorway' coming from the plateau car park, but it is quicker to climb the slope on the right where it dips, and join the broad path there. Turn right and carry on the grassy way as it winds round the cone, then fork left for the last stiff pull up to the top. There is a huge cairn, which is believed to be the remains of a burial cairn, a trig point and a splendid view.

3 To descend, retrace your steps until you reach a zigzag grassy path going off to the left from the main path. Go down it until it disappears, then look for an obvious gap in the low stone wall below you to your left. There is a clear path heading for this gap so make for it and step over the two strands of wire above the wall. Go on along the small path which crosses the shoulder called 'Wind and Weather', then it descends past an ancient square enclosure and on down to the top of a craggy ridge called 'The Devil's Burdens'. Turn left and walk along above the crags until you reach a break in the escarpment where the path goes gently down. Carry on along a small path now at the base of the slope until you reach a larger path where it comes through a gate. Turn right and follow it downhill beside a wall to join a wider path at a T-junction and turn right again.

4 The sandy path runs through heather with some boggy patches. It turns left and goes down to cross a burn, but just before it gets there look for a small path on the right which continues on the near side of the burn. This path is very wet in places at first but soon gets into drier terrain, winding among knolls. There is a fine view down the valley with cliffs on both sides. The prominent rock outcrop on the north side is called John Knox's Pulpit. Below you the burn winds through potholes and falls over shelves of rock, forming sheets of tufa over which the water slides. Go down steeply into the lower part of the valley. Wind round the side, where you may hear the 'chacking' of both stonechats and whinchats, or see them perched prominently on the heather. Eventually pass through a gate into an enclosure of young trees. The burn is now far below and the path winds round the edge of the steep slope. Carry

on past an abandoned stile and down steps to cross the burn on a good bridge. Climb steps on the far side and walk above the valley into a stand of mature deciduous trees. The path brings you down to a gate out onto the road. Turn right and return to the car park.

Whinchat

Practicals

Type of walk: *This is a steep but enjoyable climb to the highest hill in Fife. There are paths most of the way although the descent over the Devil's Burdens is not always clear and may be difficult in mist. There is an alternative route straight off the top but it is extremely steep and worn.*

Distance: 7 miles/11.3km
Time: 3–4 hours
Maps: OS Explorer 370/Landranger 58

East Lomond and Maspie Den

Park in the large car park in the centre of Falkland, grid ref 254073. To access this turn west off the A912 and drive along the main street towards the market cross. Following car park signs, turn left along Cross Wynd then left again along Horse Market. Turn left and immediately right to go past the toilets into the car park.

The Lomond Hills, whilst not particularly high, stand out spectacularly from the plains of central Fife. They are known locally as the 'Paps of Fife' because of their conical shape, rising from a high plateau. The rock is volcanic quartz-dolerite, over a base of layers of sandstone and limestone, which the igneous rock has protected from erosion.

Falkland Palace was built in the early 16th century as a hunting lodge in the royal park of Falkland, which was given to Mary of Gueldres as a wedding gift when she married James II. It is open to the public and well worth visiting.

The walks in Maspie Den, and other walks on the Falkland House estate, were created by

Falkland Palace

Margaret and Onesiphorous Tyndall Bruce. Margaret inherited the estate from her uncle in the early 19th century, and she and her husband increased the size of it, introduced new farming methods and planted many trees both for timber and for amenity. They also had the House of Falkland and the church built, and donated the village fountain.

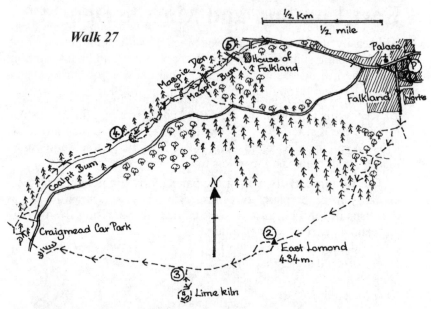

1 Go back out of the car park by the way you came in. Walk left and then right along Horse Market, and turn left at the end to go up Cross Wynd to a crossroads. Continue uphill along East Loan with the old paper works to your left, and at the end of the road carry on along a surfaced footpath, following a sign for East Lomond. Branch right at a Y-junction, then about 110yds/100m further on ascend a stepped way, on the left, following signs. Go past an enclosed water tank and up through an open area to a fine grove of mature beech trees. Cross a less distinct track and carry on up the steps, still following signs. The path then bears right along the edge of conifers and for a short while the gradient is easier, but soon it turns left again and the steep ascent up steps continues. Eventually you come out of the trees and the path swings right, making a diagonal traverse across the open hillside directly towards the conical peak of East Lomond. The slope becomes less steep as you reach the plateau and for a short distance the going is easy, then it becomes steeper again as you cross a stile and start the

94

final climb to the summit. Notice the rings round the summit cone as you go up; there was once a fort here. The remains of hut circles are still visible on top. There is also a splendid view and an excellent view indicator. The trig point is unusually situated on a much lower spur to the south.

2 To descend, leave the top by one of the three paths heading generally west. They are all steep but by zigzagging it is possible to get down fairly easily; and they all seem to be much the same, joining at the base of the volcanic summit cone. Notice the fine ditch and bank running round the hill on the way down. The path at the bottom reaches a kissing gate; go through and turn right on the well-made path beyond. Twenty metres further on go through a gate on the left to visit a lime-kiln. There are interpretive boards about the geology of the area and the way the limekilns worked. Enjoy the flowers which are influenced by the lime in the soil here; you may find northern marsh orchids, water avens, kingcups and marsh cinquefoil. Listen for curlews bub-bling in spring as they display over the high moorland, and skylarks singing.

Yellow mountain pansies

3 Return to the main track and walk left, fol-lowing the wide walled outrake between banks of bilberry. Look left into the pasture where the short grass is studded with yellow mountain pansies in spring and early summer. The track winds round between old quarries to a narrow road. Cross and walk through the car park opposite, past the toilets and out along a path at the far end signed to West Lomond. This curves round a bank to a kissing gate. Go through and in a few metres fork right along a path signed to Falkland. Cross the field to a gate, then cross the track beyond it and carry on down with larch trees to your left and re-planted clear-fell to the right. Go through a deer gate into open regenerating woodland and take the left path at the next junction. Cross the bridge over the burn and continue down the clear well-made path with fine views across the valley to East Lomond.

4 Go through another deer gate, then ignore a path on the right but take the next, clearer, one about twenty metres further on. This leads back downhill towards the Maspie Burn and then winds round on a wide shelf beneath an overhang with the burn cascading in a narrow waterfall

95

over the top. Walk on down steps on the far side to cross a bridge. The banks of the ravine, Maspie Den, are colourful with flowers in spring; wood and water avens and their hybrid line the banks, with carpets of wild strawberry and bugle. Go across three more wooden bridges, with the burn tumbling over shelves of rock beside you, then cross a stone bridge. The banks of the burn are lower here and are clothed with conifers. Take a right fork to go over another wooden bridge and cross a land-slipped area where the path has been well repaired. Walk on down to cross a wooden bridge running underneath the arch of a high stone bridge. Ignore the next stone bridge and continue through a stone-lined tunnel made through the steep bank. It curves in the middle and you may feel happier using your torch as you can't really see daylight at all, but it is level and without projections.

5   The path carries on by the burn, through mature woodland. Go under the arch of a high stone bridge with an attractive parapet, then cross the next wooden bridge to walk beneath the walls of the House of Falkland, now a school. Cross yet another bridge over the burn and come out of the wood onto a narrow road. Turn right and walk down past the stables and the lodge into Falkland. Carry straight on to the market square, go past the splendid church and walk ahead until you reach the gates of Falkland Palace. Look on the right side of the road, opposite these, for a narrow entry beside the inn, signed to 'Beer Garden'. This is a ginnel leading back to the car park. Go through, turn left and right and you are there.

Blackcap

Practicals

Type of walk: *Splendid. It combines a demanding short climb to a magnificent viewpoint with an exciting walk down a gorge. Children will love the waterfall and the tunnel, and the many varied bridges. The paths are good and mostly clear.*

Distance: 5½ miles/9km
Time: 4 hours
Maps: OS Explorer 370/Landranger 58 and 59 (part on each)

Largo Law and Keil's Den

Park on the old railway bed, at the east end of the fine viaduct (alas closed to all), at Lower Largo, grid ref 417025. Access this from the A915 then south along Harbour Wynd and left at a signed Y-junction.

Largo Kirk is delightful and walkers will enjoy the peace to be found within. Outside in the churchyard, by a gate, look for the **Pictish Largo Stone**. Part of it was found in the Largo Estate in 1839 being used as a drain cover. Today it stands in a roofed and grilled enclosure. Shade the protective glass with your hand and see if you can detect the figures and animals carved into it.

Largo Law, conical in shape, is a volcanic plug that is a great landmark along the Firth of Forth. Only one route is tolerated to the summit in this rich agricultural land. Unfortunately this is the steepest face of the hill and the erosion is bad. Try ascending and descending making your own zigzag route. It has two humps and the highest (950ft/290m) carries the cairn and trig pillar.

1 Walk out of the end of the parking area and continue along the hedged, grassy, disused railway track. Go down a few steps, cross a road and climb steps back onto the old track. Continue on to pass a Fife Coastal footpath sign and then, at the end of the houses on the left, take an unsigned grassy path. Go past a discreet sewage works to enter the

Andrew Selkirk's grave, Largo

97

Woodland Trust Reserve of Largo Serpentine Woods, where walkers are made welcome. Carry on the delightful way as it climbs above a wooded burn. At the T-junction turn left and head on along another pleasant hedged way, lined with spring flowers. Turn right to join the main road, with a fine view across to the magnificent church, Largo Kirk, on a little hill, and walk into Upper Largo. Take the next left turn, signed for church and cemetery. Turn left again immediately and make some time to visit the Kirk and wander through the churchyard to see the Largo Stone and also the gravestone commemorating Alexander Selkirk's relatives, the latter the hero of Defoe's 'Robinson Crusoe'. (Upper Largo is twinned with Robinson Crusoe Island off South America.)

Largo Law 290m ④

Pitcruvie Castle

Walk 28

Chesterstone ③

Cemetery

Upper Largo A915 A917 ②

Keil Burn

Lower Largo

Largo Burn

A915

N

½ Km ½ mile

2 Leave the church and return a few steps along your approach road and then stroll left along a narrow road to rejoin the road to the cemetery. Turn left and walk up past the school, and then right at the cemetery. Pass through a small car park and a kissing gate. To the left rears Largo Law. Walk on along a grassy track beside a huge field and wind left to reach a cottage where you turn right before it. Go through an open gateway – if the gate is closed over the track a notice tells you to climb it. Walk on towards Chesterstone farm and turn left, as directed, before a huge barn. Wind right and then left again, as signed, and climb steadily a wide track, hedged and fenced. Go past a tall wind turbine and then on through a large gate or climb the stile beside it and continue steadily up to the foot of the Law.

3 From now on the path is very steep for more than half of your climb. Pause often to enjoy the views. Eventually you reach a narrow level

area where you can take a little break to get your breath back. Carry on up where the path is easier to climb to find three paths continuing on, all which reach the first summit, 758ft/283m. Then descend on another good path to a grassy valley to climb a stile and go on up a steep but good path that leads to the highest point on the Law. Here there is a trig point and, to the left, a cairn. The grassy slopes are very pleasant and in spring support wood anemones and celandines. Find a sheltered corner to have your lunch and wander around to enjoy the superb views and perhaps spot kestrel, sparrowhawk, buzzard and many skylarks.

4   Descend by your upward route, which is even harder in some parts and where you might wish to make a diversion to the left and then back again to avoid the worst parts. Follow your outward route to the cemetery. Go through the gate on the right into the cemetery and climb gently to leave by a gate just before a small building, on the left, onto the road. Cross to walk a footpath stretching ahead, with a fine wall to your left. There is a sign at the beginning that says 'No dogs'. Go through a kissing gate and walk through two more gates close together. Look left whilst between these two to see an old tower later used as a doocot. Then go through another gate to pass a caravan site on the right to reach another gate. Enjoy the stunning views of the Firth ahead.

5   Cross the next road and take the small footpath opposite, signed Keil's Den, between planted fields. Then pass through a gap in the fence and turn right onto path that takes you along the rim of Keil's Den, passing through splendid deciduous woodland where the ground, in spring, is carpeted with bluebells and wood anemones. Listen for willow warbler, chiffchaff, blackcap and garden warbler as you walk. Down in the deep den wild cherry grows in profusion. On reaching Keil Burn you may have to climb the shallow steps to the road and then descend more steps at the end of the bridge to rejoin the charming path. On approaching the edge of the woodland, curve round left to stroll a boardwalk and continue on, remaining very high above the burn. Eventually you may wish to descend a path down to the side of the burn and stroll on. The high path and the path by the river join before a gate to emerge from the lovely woodland onto a good path beside an enormous field to the right and a hedge to the left. Carry on ahead to reach the road.

Red grouse

6 Turn left, cross the bridge and dawdle on until you reach the rather busy A915. Wind left and remain on the pavement until you can take a right turn, Harbour Wynd. Descend the road and take a signed left turn at a Y-junction. This leads to the car park at the end of the splendid viaduct that once carried the railway line, now used for parking.

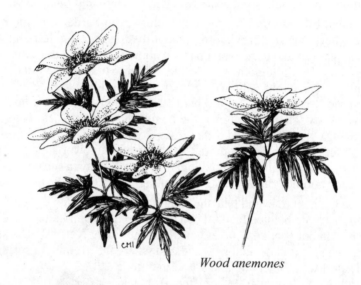

Wood anemones

Practicals

Type of walk: *After visiting the delightful church this route climbs Largo Law, very steep in parts, but not particularly high. If you find it too difficult (after rain) be prepared to turn back and continue on the lovely way through Keil's Den – a splendid walk in itself.*

Distance: 6 miles/9.5km

Time: 3–4 hours

Map: OS Explorer 370/Landranger 59

Walk 29

Elie and Kilconquhar Loch

Park on either side of the road, grid ref 492001, in front of Elie Church, which dates back to the 17th century.

The villages of **Elie and Earlsferry** stretch for a mile along a lovely south facing bay which has rocky projections at either end. Earlsferry, along the western half of the bay, became a Royal burgh in 1373 and an important port but was unable to operate after 1766 when a great storm filled its harbour with sand. Elie, lying along the eastern half of the bay and better protected from storms, then came into its own as a good port.

Male **eiders** are handsome black and white birds, their mates are brown barred with black. As they congregate in groups the drakes utter low coos, a delight to hear. Look for them on the sea, often close to rocks where they hunt for molluscs or crustaceans in weeds. The nest, constructed of grass, heather or seaweed, is often found in the open or under the shelter of a wall or rock.

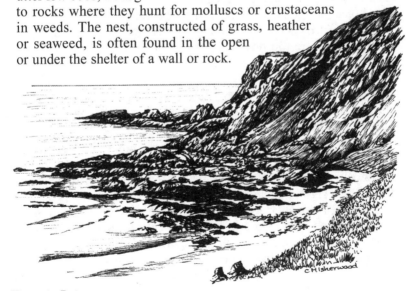

Kincraig Point

101

The duck lays at least five large greenish eggs after lining her nest with down. Once female eiders were exploited by man. The down was stolen from the nest and used for eiderdowns. This left the duck having to line her nest again.

Walk 29

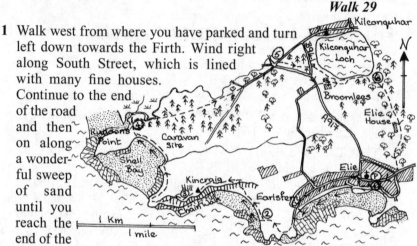

1 Walk west from where you have parked and turn left down towards the Firth. Wind right along South Street, which is lined with many fine houses. Continue to the end of the road and then on along a wonderful sweep of sand until you reach the end of the massive retaining sea wall at Earlsferry to take steps up onto the road – you might have to use the latter to avoid the sands if the tide is high. Turn left to walk past more houses and then out onto green sward and more of the Fife Coastal Path, which runs beside the wall of a sturdily built house on the right. Here in this open area, in April, the rough grass of the cliffs is bright with scurvy grass and an enormous number of cowslips. Here too flower thrift and ground ivy. Look out to sea where you might spot mergansers, long tailed duck and hear and see eiders. Wind round with the wall of the house and then, descend beside it. Where the wall turns away right, drop down the track, with golf links on either side where you should watch out for balls. On joining a track, turn left and walk down to the shore. Here walk right.

2 If tide is high there is a path, marked with red posts, through the lyme and marram grass just above the shore. Otherwise wind round the bay on the lovely sands to a short flight of steps up through the shallow dunes. Turn right at the top and take a few steps, to a signpost, where the two paths meet. Here begin your long ascent of Kincraig Hill, climbing stone steps, close together and easy to manage. The way is railed until you reach a seat on the right. More steps go on up to the cliff top where there are remnants of wartime installations and from where there is a stunning view. Turn left and walk, with care, along the continuing narrow path, which soon passes through a fenced area

around the remains of some wartime lookouts. Here grow masses of cowslips and meadow saxifrage. A peregrine uses an old mast for its lookout post. Beyond is the trig point.

3 Carry on down the good path to reach two bench seats and a fine view of the sea on both sides of the promontory. After a pause descend steps and walk a fine stretch of the path. Wind on round to Shell Bay, where the path edges a huge field, with the sea to your left. Head on to cross a flat plank bridge to reach the corner of a caravan and chalet site. Here you may be able to continue along the shore, or if the tide is high, Coastal Way markers guide you parallel with the shore and on the green sward just above the caravans. Both routes bring you to the end of the holiday park and to the beginning of a short wide sandy track through a very obvious gap in an extensive shelterbelt of Scots pine. Here you leave the Coastal Way.

4 Turn right immediately beyond the pines and stride the good path. Eventually you reach a cross of tracks. Press on along the track ahead through a vast pine forest. Beside the track is a wide unturfed track, which acts as a firebreak. Keep ahead through the forest and then the path narrows as it leads you through pleasing decidu-

Meadow saxifrage

ous woodland and on to the access road to the caravan park. Use the well kept verges of this road as you walk left, to reach the A917. Cross and walk a short way along the unclassified road opposite to take an unobtrusive gap into the forest on your right. It is not signed but asks you to 'take your litter home'. There is also a log across the path.

5 Walk ahead through the trees. The path is indistinct in places. Keep roughly parallel with the A-road to your right, which you will hear rather than see. If you drift towards it you might lose the path, but the woodland floor is very easy to walk. Eventually a grassy, reinforced track leads below some large laurel bushes and onto the B941. Cross and walk right along a pleasing path that keeps well away from the A-road for a time and then the pavement continues for a short way beside the road to the left turn, signed Broomlees, which you take. Walk the quiet way to pass cottages and then between large barns.

Follow the track as it continues beside woodland on your left through which you can spot Kilconquhar Loch. Stride the pleasing track as it curves left into the trees and carries on parallel with the loch where you might spot coot and tufted duck.

6 Press on, ignoring any side turns to pass magnificent Elie House, now being converted into flats and town houses. Stroll on and at the A917 turn right to walk into Elie.

Peregine

Practicals

Type of walk: *Delightful. Beach walk, cliff top walk, woodland walk.*

Distance: 8 miles/13km
Time: 4 hours
Maps: OS Explorer 371/Landranger 59

Walk 30

Elie to St Monans

Park at Ruby Bay car park at East Links, Elie, grid ref 497997. Access this from the A917 by a narrow road (east), north of Elie. Car parks on the Coastal Path have bus stops for those who wish to walk one way and return by public transport.

Lady Janet Anstruther, wife of the laird of Ardross and Elie estate, built the Lady's Tower at Ruby Bay in the late 18th century as her summerhouse. She enjoyed bathing naked in the sea and sent a bell-ringer around the village each time she went swimming to warn townsfolk to keep away. She also had the hamlet of Balclevie removed in 1771 to improve her view from Elie House. A local fortune-teller is said to have cursed the Anstruthers because of this, saying that only six generations of the family would live in the house. Her prediction came true.

Newark Castle

St Monans Parish church is one of the oldest in use in Scotland and is reputed to be the closest to the sea. The church was built on the site of a shrine established around the ninth century when Irish clergy fled to Scotland, bringing with them the relics of St Monan.

1 From the car park at Ruby Bay, named after the Elie 'rubies' (pieces of clear red garnet that can sometimes be found on the bay's unusual volcanic sand) follow the path, north, through a grassy area named Shepherd's Knowe, which in early summer is colourful with cowslips. Head on along a narrow path leading off the main one to visit Elie lighthouse, built in 1908 to the designs of David Stevenson of the famous lighthouse family. Then go on to the ruinous Lady's Tower, which Lady Anstruther used as her summerhouse. Listen and look for linnets, meadow pipits and skylarks here.

Walk 30

2 Carry on along the sandy shoreline. The dunes to the left are held in place by marram grass. At low tide ragged reefs stretch out towards the sea. Go on to pass the ruinous Ardross Castle, built in 1370. From here see if you can spot, inland, a rectangular doocot, where pigeons were housed throughout the winter to provide food for the inhabitants of the castle during the coldest months.

Cowslips

3 Press on along the path to pass a 'filled in' railway bridge and to wind round a bay. Enjoy the dramatic views from here, both north and south. Stroll on, with another castle coming into view. This is Newark Castle, built in the 15th century for the Sandilands family. It stands on a fine promontory overlooking the sea and is

approached by steps. Follow the waymark directions carefully because the path has been slightly diverted.

4 From the castle you may have to make a high tide diversion. Look for the notice on a post on the shore, warning that if the tide has reached a certain height up the post you need to take the alternative route. This heads inland on a track and then, before a house, winds right to run along a field edge before crossing a small bridge over St Monans burn. It then rejoins the low tide route near the historical church of St Monan.

5 Just beyond Newark Castle, follow the path to another ruin, a beehive-shaped tower, close to the edge of the cliffs. This is a 16th century doocot. Then, if the tide allows, continue downhill towards the shore and on to a gate to visit the church by rounding its outer wall. From here, carry on into the attractive village. After exploration you may wish to take a bus back to the start of your walk or return by the same route to the car park.

Linnet

Practicals

Type of walk: *Delightful and full of interest.*

Distance: 6 miles/9.5km or 3 miles/5km one way
Time: 2 or 4 hours
Maps: OS Explorer 371/Landranger 59

Crail and the Fife Coastal Path

Park in Main Street, Crail, grid ref 613076, where there are many spaces to leave your vehicle.

Crail has a picturesque small harbour dating from the 16th century. It has a curved breakwater, which gives it protection against the sometimes 'aggressive' Forth. In 1826 the straight pier was added, designed by Robert Stevenson the grandfather of the author Robert Louis Stevenson.

The **Blue Stane** (stone) stands beside the church gate. According to legend it was thrown from the Isle of May by the Devil in order to damage Crail Church. The stone split in mid-air, a piece landing on Balcomie Beach near Fife Ness, the most easterly point of Fife. Behind the church is a 19th century morthouse, where bodies waiting burial

Constantine's
Cave, Fife Ness

were locked away for several weeks to deter body snatchers who sold them to University anatomists.

1 Walk south-west along Main Street and turn left down narrow, curving Shoregate to reach the stunning small harbour. After a pause here return along Shoregate for a few steps to the sharp bend, left, and go ahead up steps to the wall of Crail House (which stands where the Castle once stood). Wind right along Castle Walk, enjoying the magnificent views across the sea and of the Isle of May. Continue on the good path to reach the watch house and descend right just beyond. This

Walk 31

excellent tarmacked path takes you down the slope and then winds left just above the sea. Carry on the lovely way to join the continuing Fife Coastal Path, a reinforced track, just above boulders, reefs and masses of seaweed revealed by the receding tide. Head on the grassy top of the sea wall. Go past a white doocot, built in the 16th century. Stroll on along the edge of Roome Bay passing a delightful pool where children dabble with nets. Climb steps to wind round a low cliff slippage to continue on a tarmac road through a caravan park, just above the shore. Curve round with the road as it passes between many chalets and then a dirt path continues with scurvy grass, in spring, growing in profusion and perfuming the air.

2 Go on through a kissing gate into Kilminning Coast Willdlife Reserve. Ahead lies an intriguing stack and many boulders known as Kilminning Castle where you might wish to take a little pause. Look for seals out at sea and gannets flying fast, straight ahead, before diving for fish. You might also see fulmars and cormorants. The green sward is spangled with primroses and on the bank to your left grows an enormous mass

Primrose

of gorse, heavily laden with blossom, where linnets nest and you might also spot a reed bunting. As you near an old wartime gun emplacement the path climbs up and then descends as it passes through gorse on one side and a large mass of blackthorn, covered in white flowers on the other.

3   Press on to go over a natural rock dyke ascending and then descending easy steps. Stroll on to leave the Reserve and continue past a large barn-like building. Beyond stands the imposing Coastguard Station and its tall mast at Fife Ness. Wind round the latter to join a narrow road. Pass several caravans and a cottage at what was once Fife Harbour, a treacherous place for landing a boat. A plaque here says that this is where Mary of Guise landed on her way to St Andrews to marry James V. Then take a narrow path leading, right, to look at a tidal mill, with another interesting plaque. Return to the little road and here, in early summer, look and listen for whitethroats. Almost immediately take the waymarked path going off right, to carry on along the foot of Craighead golf course. White posts mark the edge of the course and boards warn you that flying golf balls are very dangerous and to stand still when someone is taking a shot.

4   From now on the way runs along the narrow path or sends you down onto the sands below. These are very pleasant to walk and safer too. Go on past Constantine's large cave, where legend has it that the king was killed (874) by raiding Danes. Stroll on below Balcomie golf course where a multitude of cowslips flower. Look left from here to see in the distance, Balcomie Castle and its outbuildings, now a farm. It is near here, at the end of the sand, that the other part of the Blue Stane is thought to have landed. When you reach the end of the course and a

110

farm gate, locked and wired, leave the Coastal Path, turn left and climb a narrow trod beside the fence on your right. Wind round right at the top and join a wide farm track, with grass running down the middle. This climbs gently, quite straight between huge arable fields. Pass a large house with a strong gate and go on by Wormiston farm. Soon after, the wide track becomes a metalled road and continues uphill.

5 Where the road swings right, go ahead on a similar wide track used by cyclists. Wind round left with it and then when opposite some derelict buildings, turn right along another wider, easier track to walk. As it nears the outskirts of Crail go past a well-concealed caravan site and then follow the track beside it on your left. Turn right to go past a new cemetery and then turn left before the fine church and its churchyard, to follow a delightful path down through Denburn Wood. Cross a footbridge and carry on the path. Cross the next bridge and climb the path to the road. Turn right to walk up Marketgate to pass the church, which is well worth a visit. Press on along Main Street to where you have parked.

Eiders

Practicals

Type of walk: *Very pleasant. Along shore paths and fields tracks. Take care as you pass the golf course.*

Distance: 7 miles/11.4km
Time: 4 hours
Maps: OS Explorer 371/Landranger 59

Walk 32

Cambo and Kingsbarns

Park in the layby just before Cambo Lodge, grid ref 599106, on the west side of the A917, south of Kingsbarns Village.

Cambo Estate lies close to the village of Kingsbarns. The 19th century Cambo House is the home of Sir Peter and Lady Erskine. The gardens are open to the public. Elsewhere on the estate is the Kingsbarns Links golf course and also fine walks, free to the public, through fine deciduous woodland. The old house comprised a tower house with many additions. It was destroyed by fire in 1875 after a staff party when the Erskine family were away. The present grand house was built on the same site between 1879 and 1884.

Snowdrops flower from January to March and the flower is open from about ten to four o'clock. The woodland floor over which this walk passes supports a huge number of these lovely flowers and is a wonderful sight, promising that spring cannot be too far ahead.

Remains of Kingsbarns Harbour

1 Cross the busy road with care and walk left along the pavement inside the safety barrier to reach the fine gates to Cambo. Turn left just inside, keeping to the right of the lodge on the left, to take an easy-to-miss unsigned footpath which runs behind it. Walk on along the narrow path through woodland crossing small boards over tiny streams. Carry on through beech woodland, delightful in spring and glorious in autumn. Cross a track and go on through a gate with a 'walkers welcome' sign. Look to the right of this

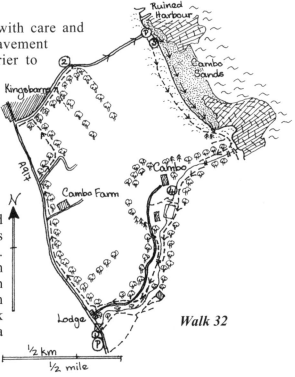

Walk 32

long belt of trees to see a huge arable field. Cross the narrow access track to Cambo farm and take the next gate to walk beside a pretty pond, with a sturdy wall to your left. Cross a road and stroll on through more mixed woodland where, as you go, you might spot yellowhammer, blue tit, robin, wren and maybe a pair of bullfinches devouring the seeds of an elm tree. Continue on the narrow path to come to a gate to a road and the village of Kingsbarns. Do not leave the wood here. Turn right and carry on along the path that continues through more open deciduous woodland.

2 At the end of the woodland, where the path and the wood swing right, turn left to go through a gate onto Sea Road. Turn right and walk down the walled way, with a golf course on one side and a large arable fields to your left where you might spot partridges. Press on down

Grey partridges

113

to the large parking area on the shore. There are picnic tables here, a large wooden shelter and toilets. Take either of the grassy paths on each side of the shelter to reach the sands and look for the fascinating remnants of the old Kingsbarns harbour.

3 Turn right out of the car park to join the Coastal Way to walk a sandy track well above the beach. Or if the tide is out go down through a gate from the car park, on to the shore, and walk right along the extensive wonderful sands. When you can spot Scots pines above the shallow dunes, follow a narrow grassy path on the shore side of the trees that leads onto a road, part of the golf course. Wind round right, ignore two footbridges over the Cambo burn, and take the wide path into the delectable mainly sycamore woodland, with the Cambo burn, in its narrow bed, to your left. Ignore the next bridge, and the steps beyond over the burn, and take the farther bridge with fewer steps to climb above the ravine.

4 From the gently climbing path you can look down on the burn tumbling through its ravine. Carry on to spot Cambo House through the trees. Go through a gateless opening in an old wall and walk through a small garden. Move on into pleasing woodland to look down on the estate's fine vegetable garden. Pass through a gated gap in a wall into a wilder section. Cross the replacement bridge and turn left to walk on through the glorious woodland. Pass below dramatic sandstone cliffs on the other side of the narrow burn. Head on along duckboarding and then at a footbridge, ignore the waymarks to walk ahead uphill. Go over the access route to Cambo House and into more woodland. Follow the path, left, to come out at the lodge by the ornamental gates from where you started this delightful walk.

Practicals

Type of walk: *Very pleasing. The first section of path could be muddy. Well waymarked with Woodland Trust markers through much of the woodland. Glorious sandy beach.*

Distance: 4 miles/6.5km
Time: 2–3 hours
Maps: OS Explorer 371/Landranger 59

St Andrews

Park in Abbey Street, near to the junction with South Street, St Andrews, grid ref 512166. If this is full there are many other places to park.

The town is named after **St Andrew**, the apostle. Its famous beautiful cathedral, the largest in Scotland, now lies in ruins. Construction started in 1158 and continued for over a century. It was damaged by storm in the 13th century and by fire in the 14th. In 1559 it was stripped of its altar and all its images. By the end of the 16th century more of it collapsed and much stone was taken away for other buildings. Prominent on the lovely site is the tower of St Rule, built of grey sandstone, it predates the cathedral and may have been built to hold the relics of St Andrew.

The ruins of **St Andrews Castle** stand on a cliff top looking out over the North Sea. It was first built around 1200 as a home for bishops and later for archbishops. It

St Andrews Cathedral

was also used as a prison and a fortress. Then later, after bits were demolished and other parts rebuilt, what you see dates back to the middle 1500s. Much of its stone was used to build the harbour.

1 Leave Abbey Street and turn left along South Street. Go left into Queens Gardens, then right into Queens Terrace. Where the latter winds right, stroll a ginnel, on the left, Lade Braes walk, a walled track. Continue on the Lade Way, shadowed by houses and high walls. Cross a busy road by the pedestrian crossing and continue along the Lade Way. When you reach a car park on the right, turn left, down Viaduct Walk, a tree-lined track crossing the Kinness Burn. At its end join Canongate and continue right.

2 Remain on the pavement to pass the car park for the impressive Botanic Gardens, which you might wish to visit, and then carry on along the road to pass Canongate Primary School with its huge playing field, which interests a large number of rooks and jackdaws. Beyond the school, head right down Maynard Road. At the end of the houses the road narrows to a path and descends steeply between fine forest trees to reach Kinness Burn, which flows through the centre of the town into the sea at the harbour. Cross the bridge over the pretty stream and bear left along Lade Braes Walk. At a red pantiled cottage, once New Mill, curve left and press on above the burn. Then the path moves away from the stream above wide green slopes down to your left with woodland climbing upwards on the right.

3 Cross another bridge over the burn and continue ahead then left ascending a gravelled path that climbs beside woodland, on the left, and with the green sward of Hallow Hill to the right. As you approach several lofty horsechestnut trees climb, right, up the slope and wind round beside trees, on the left, to a plaque. This describes a Pictish cemetery that covered the hill between the 5th

Walk 33

116

and 9th centuries AD. Beside the plaque are traces of stone-lined graves. Then go on downhill towards the first house of an estate to curve left to walk beside the Cairnsmill Burn. Cross a footbridge over the hurrying water and walk on right along the opposite side of it, below the hill and through quiet woodland.

4 Look left of the next bridge to see a stone weir across the burn controlling the flow. Growing all around this pleasing corner are many plants of blue lettuce, in flower in June. Turn right beyond the bridge and stride along a reinforced track with the burn to your right and hedged gardens to your left and many deciduous trees overhanging the gurgling stream. This leads you to a fine pond (mill pond) surrounded by trees. Sit here by the pretty red-roofed small building, part of Law Mill which ceased working in 1905, and watch children feed the mallards. Go on past a house, below on the right, with an ancient waterwheel still in place. The Law Mill belonged to the Priory and was probably built in the 13th century and used for fulling cloth to tighten the weave. Cross the bridge over the Kinness Burn and turn right to reach your outward path by the grassy area.

Blue lettuce

5 Go on past the 'New Mill' to continue on the Lade Braes walk taken earlier. A short way along, beyond the bridge you crossed on the way in, notice a path dropping down to the side of the burn. Walk this fine way, close to the water, to where it climbs to meet the high-level one just before a children's play area at the start of King George V fields. Go ahead soon to pass the gates to the park, cross the road and wind right to walk between houses. Walk on along the track, still on Lade Braes walk, until you reach the start of the Viaduct Walk taken earlier.

6 This time turn left to go through the long narrow car park to Argyle Street and turn right to cross a road and walk through an arch, West Port, once an entrance or a gate to the town. Keep on the left side of the continuing road, South Street, and soon look across to the shell of an ancient church, all that remains of Blackfriars Monastery. Just before

Holy Trinity church, turn left down a narrow road, Logie's Lane, to join Market Street, which is full of interesting shops. Cross and walk right to take the first left up College Street. Go over North Street and up Butts Wynd to head right along The Scores to reach the ruins of the Castle.

7 Carry on along the delightful high-level railed path, with an extensive view over the North Sea where you might spot many eiders and their young and gannets diving for fish. Head on to descend gently to the harbour and walk out on the pier. Return and dawdle left along The Shore and pass through an arch on the right, Mill Port, which gives entrance to Pends Road. Climb the slope to pass through two more arches, The Pends. Continue until you can go through the entrance to the ruined St Andrew's Cathedral and Priory. After your visit, head back along South Street and turn left into Abbey Street where you have parked.

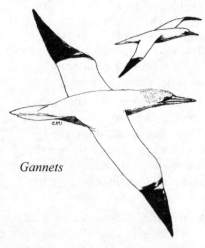

Gannets

Practicals

Type of Walk: *A superb walk through the lovely town of St Andrews, enjoying a fine riverside walk and then out to the coast to explore the Castle, the Cathedral and Priory, and the harbour.*

Distance: 3 miles/5km
Time: 2–3 hours
Maps: OS Explorer 371/Landranger 59

Walk 34

Cupar, Hill of Tarvit Mansion and Ceres

Park in one of several parking areas close to the Cupar Cemetery, grid ref 378136. This Cemetery lies on the southern edge of the town. Access it by A914 from the centre of the town and then almost immediately take the unclassified road in the direction of Ceres.

The **Hill of Tarvit Mansion House** was originally built on the site known as Wemysshall. Sir Robert Lorimer, one of Scotland's most famous architects, remodelled the house in 1906. It has beautiful gardens and if you have time on your walk you may wish to visit.

Ceres is a historic, picturesque village, with its own village green. At the other side of the Bishop's Bridge stands a **three-foot high stone carved figure** set in a 12 foot pillared structure. It is believed to have been sculpted, in the 19th century, to represent a former church provost. It was found in an overgrown garden of a nearby house. After renovation it was placed in the village in 1939.

Bishop's Bridge, Ceres

119

1 From the parking area, cross the main road and turn right to walk beside the walled woodland on your left. At the bend locate the signed footpath, 'Old Road to Ceres' and cross at a safe place. Follow the track up through deciduous Owlet Wood. It climbs easily but can be muddy underfoot. At the top of the hill, carry on beside woodland, on the right, and pastures to the left. The path is easy to walk and grassy; again it is wet in places but these are generally easy to negotiate. Go through a gate and begin a gentle descent on a narrow path bordered with many colourful flowers in mid-summer. Part way down look for a gap in the hedge, on the right, that gives access to a wide track at the top side of a huge arable field. Follow it, climbing steadily, with a fine view down to Ceres, which will be visited later on this walk. Pause to look east to see across the woodland at Tentsmuir (walk 37) and across the Tay to the faint outline of Seaton Cliffs (walk 40). Follow the track as it continues beside a walled wood. Go through a gate and pass three cottages at Whitehill farm. Wind round with the now tarmacked way to pass the farmhouse on your right. Descend the long track, with red poppies flowering in the arable fields to your left, to reach Wemysshall road and turn right.

2 Continue for a third of a mile to turn right into the entrance drive of Hill of Tarvit House. A notice board close by tells you where to get the key if, later on, you wish to enter Scotstarvit Tower, L-shaped and five storeys high, built between 1550 and 1579. Carry on up the metalled drive and wind round left with it from where you can see parts of the lovely gardens. Go past, on your right, a parking area where there are picnic tables. Stroll on along the carriageway to reach A916 and cross with care to stride the long access track to Scotstarvit Tower. As you go enjoy the view across the countryside to the Lomond Hills. After circling the tower, and maybe climbing it, return to cross the A-road and walk a short way down the drive again.

3 Just after a board reminding you to be aware of golf balls, take a gate on the right to walk a grassy path with a fence to the right – the Millennium walk. Follow the path, left, from where you can see the fine house, then walk

120

on through woodland. Follow the path where it bears right to reach a doocot, the openings for the pigeons are round the back. Then go on from here through the glorious deciduous woodland, down steps and winding left, soon to walk beside more of the golf course. Eventually you arrive at the entrance gate. Beyond, turn right and walk up the road for ⅛ mile. Cross and descend a wide track on the left. Pass the farm buildings of Wemyss Hall Mains, on the left, and continue down to a splendid packhorse bridge over the Craigrothie Burn.

4 Climb the slope beyond and wind round, acute left, with a doocot on the right, to walk a little way along. Here a tiny sign on left, directs you up a hedged track, on the right, another old road to Ceres. This pleasing way could be muddy after rain. Cross the B939 and go ahead up a tarmacked road to Denhead farm. Wind right and then left to pass three cottages and go on along the tree and hedge-lined track. Carry on along the continuing grassy way lined with a myriad of wild flowers. Descend past houses to Ceres. Cross the road and walk ahead to go over the fine Bishop's Bridge. Bear left and walk through the village, noting the pleasing houses, the sculpture of The Provost and then, beyond the B939, the Church. Go on along the road for another half mile to where it winds right for Cupar. Here go straight ahead. After passing several houses the tarmac ends and you continue on a hedged path, soon to pass the left turn, through the hedge, taken almost at the start of the walk. Press on up where you walked before, over the hill and then descend through Owlet Wood to the road. Cross with care and walk on to re-cross by the cemetery gates to where you have parked.

Yellowhammer

Practicals

Type of walk: *A very pleasant walk through quiet rolling countryside. Much interest along the way.*

Distance: 7 ½ miles/12km
Time: 4 hours
Maps: OS Explorer 370/ Landranger 59

Walk 35

Norman's Law

Park in the small village of Luthrie, where there is parking in front of the village hall, grid ref 331197. Access this by the A92 running south-west from the Tay Bridge towards Ladybank. Leave the latter by a signposted unclassified road, north, for the attractive village.

This impressive hill, **Norman's Law**, lies at the eastern end of the Ochils on the south side of the River Tay. Although not very high (936ft/285m) its position, higher than all the surrounding hills, means that it is a superb viewpoint. It is composed of volcanic rock (like the rest of the Ochils), which creates a relatively dry soil. On the summit stand a trig point, view indicator and a tumbled cairn re-shaped as a windbreak. Around this attractive top are the remains of an Iron Age fort and settlement from where the inhabitants had wide views of attackers; the hill's steep slopes also gave the folk living on top a good defensive advantage. On a clear day look for the Pentland Hills to the south, Lochnagar and Ben Macdui to the north, and Crianlarich's Ben More to the west.

Norman's Law

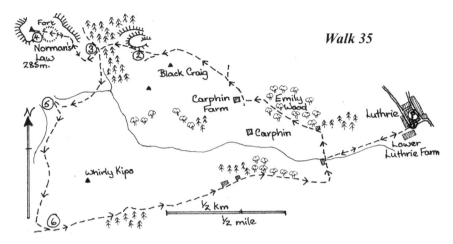

1 Leave the parking area by a passageway between houses to drop down to the unclassified road and turn left. A short way along, walk right as directed by the signpost for Norman's Law. Go past Lower Luthrie farm and continue up the long wide tree-lined track to reach a T-junction in front of a bungalow. Turn right as directed by the signpost and continue climbing, soon curving left on the good track in front of a small house. Head on along the edge of a wood, scattering many pheasants as you go. Then by another house, follow the signed main track as it bends right to pass between wooded hillocks. At the next Y-junction bear left and climb to a gate. The track carries on, pleasingly grassed in parts, moving out onto rough open pasture with scattered gorse.

2 When you reach a wet part of the track, move right to pick up an indistinct grassy way, on the right, heading towards the now visible summit of Norman's Law. Stroll on walking below a rocky hillock to the right. Eventually the path, winds left to keep beside a fence, and descends through bracken with pine woodland on both sides, to reach a metal gate giving access to a wide track.

3 Cross and climb up the banking ahead to reach a steepish path ascending the lower heathery rocky shoulder of the Law. The path is naturally stepped and a joy to climb. It brings you to a grassy stretch, which continues easily giving your legs a little respite before it reaches another short rocky way up. This leads to a long glorious grassy path that takes you across the fine plateau to the summit (936ft/285m) to enjoy the 360 degree view. Here use the view finder to identify some of the tops you can see. Close by is the trig point and a collapsed cairn that has been roughly rebuilt in the shape of a windbreak.

123

Pheasant (cock)

4 Return down the way of your ascent to reach the gate. Here go through if you wish to make a quick and easy return to Luthrie. For a more difficult but pleasing way back, turn right along the track and continue on a rather wet way (after heavy rain) to a gate. Beyond is a good track, which suddenly becomes an indistinct narrow path through long grass below Norman's Law's western slope. Keep parallel, but away from, the boundary fence on your right. Eventually the path swings right to come beside the fence where a large black arrow on a white board directs you hard left through even longer grass.

5 A very slight indentation of the grass after a gorse bush, denotes the start of the path, which is very narrow and sunken. It wanders about a bit but finally brings you, after bearing a little right, to another gate in a fence, similarly marked. Stride ahead over the next pasture to another arrowed gate to join a wide grassy track, which runs below Whirly Kips, with Denmuir farm away to the right. The track disappears for a very short way and then reappears once more. Curve round left with the track below the hill on your left and go ahead over a stile to join a wide track which comes in on the right. Go through an old gate across the way.

Red squirrel

124

6 From now on the 1¼ mile track takes you through the pleasing countryside. It climbs, it passes through small sections of woodland and strides between pastures. It is easy to walk. Look for a picturesque view of the Law, through the trees on your left. It then passes some pretty cottages at Wester Kinsleith and as you continue look left to see Carphin and its doocot. Finally the long track makes a wide swing left and comes to the bungalow and the entrance gates to Carphin, reached early on in the walk. Turn right to return down the track to pass Lower Luthrie farm. At the road turn left and then right up the ginnel to the parking area.

*Red Admiral, Bell
heather and lichens*

Practicals

Type of walk: *Good tracks and paths for most of the way to the wonderful top, with its panoramic view. The return route has a tiresome stretch across two pastures of long grass (in autumn) where the path is sometimes difficult to find. In spite of this it is always pleasing to return by a different route though returning by your outward way is a delight.*

Distance: 5½ miles/9km
Time: 3–4 hours
Maps: OS Explorer 370/Landranger 59

Walk 36

Fife Coastal Path from Balmerino

Park in a small layby on the left, just before Balmerino Mill, grid ref 357249. To access this turn off the B946, west, about 1 mile south of Wormit and at the Y-junction take the right fork signed for Balmerino. Another right turn leads to the village. After passing the signed Balmerino Abbey, where the narrow road swings right, go straight ahead down a track.

Today the ruins of **Balmerino Abbey** are to be found in an idyllic tranquil corner of the village where you will want to linger. Once it was a very busy place, home to a community of hard working monks and part of a European network of monasteries. In 1660 the abbey was incorporated into a private dwelling and this helped the ruins you see today to survive.

Balmerino Abbey

The **Tay rail bridge** strides 2½ miles across the Firth from Dundee to Wormit in Fife. It was completed in early 1878 and opened June 1, 1878. On the night of December 28, 1879 the bridge collapsed during a severe winter gale. Six carriages, 75 passengers and crew plunged into the icy waters and died. During construction of the bridge the effect of high winds had not been allowed for. A new double-track bridge was opened on July 13, 1887. The piers of the original bridge are still visible above the river even at high tide. A hundred metric tons of bird droppings were scraped off the ironwork lattice using hand tools.

1 Walk towards the shore of the Firth of Tay, following the Fife Coastal Path (FCP) waymark past the disused mill, now a private house. Wind right on the wide track to pass in front of several charming cottages. Continue with a fence to the right and with the Firth lapping up against the track on your left. Carry on through Nether Kirkton where the track runs a little left between the houses and the shore. Here dogs must be on a lead. Look across the Tay to see Dundee with the Sidlaw Hills beyond. Climb the path, with arable land to the right and a hedge to your left now obscuring your view of the Tay. Go through a gate into woodland, the path climbing gently, high above the shore.

2 Take the signed long easy flight of steps up through the trees and turn left to continue on a much higher path. Eventually the young trees to the right are left behind and an arable field comes right down to the side of the path. (You will be able to spot this on your return, by several posts with white discs along the edge of the path). Forest trees to your left allow a few glimpses of the shore below. Stroll on through a short stretch of woodland to pass through a kissing gate.

3 Follow the signposted way beside rough ground to reach a flight of steps down to a plank bridge over a little stream. Then climb again, soon to descend once more to step over

Walk 36

another small stream. Pause along the way to look down through a gap in the trees on the now very wide Firth to a shipwreck below. Continue on the narrow path across a sloping rough pasture with a wide open view across the Tay, past dense gorse to your right. The way opens out even more and you have a view of the entire Tay rail bridge striding across the wide estuary, over which cross seemingly toy trains. You might even spot the elegant road bridge beyond. Sit on the seat by the path, a carved wooden seal, for your first break and enjoy the view, including Wormit village snuggling into its hillside. Follow the path as it begins to descend and comes to a kissing gate into woodland. Branches of blackthorn arc overhead and then the path brings you down to the shore. Look for curlews probing the mud for food and wind right round Wormit Bay on a low path beside the water.

4 Before the first house take the signposted path on the right and climb a narrow path beside an arable field. Follow the path as it rises above a pond on the left where a pair of swans patrol with their cygnets. At the end of the pond a narrow steep path drops to a wooden stile over a barbed fence. Ignore this path and carry on ahead along a short narrow path, which is sometimes overgrown with lush summer vegetation, to reach a huge arable field.

5 Turn right and climb the right of way along the edge of the growing crop or in autumn through the stubble (the route way is clearer at such a time). Keep up over the ridge and on up and up. Then curve steadily left to climb the huge pasture towards a row of telegraph poles and to reach a gap in the low vegetation of the boundary. Go through the gap and walk right to the waymarked corner. Turn left and stroll beside the hedge on your right. Turn round the next corner and follow the path up to the obvious signpost. Follow the track, right, and wind round between two large barns of Peacehill farm, to a T-junction of tracks where you turn left. A short way along, leave the main track and walk right, keeping beside a hedge on your right. Carry on along the pleasant way until you reach two more large barns.

6 Turn right before the barns, along a delightful track, as it passes through more fields. At the next T-junction bear left and walk on. Once past Kilburns and several cottages, go ahead on a narrow path, next to the hedge, keeping it immediately on your left. Follow the path with superb views down to the Firth. (The posts, with white discs mentioned above, lie between you and the Tay.) Follow the path into deciduous woodland. After rain this can be a rather wet way, partly because it is used by horses-riders; however you can edge round and in between the wettest areas. Eventually the path brings you to a hedged slope, down

right, beside a house and then left along a track to reach a narrow road. Cross and strike slightly right to walk below the houses of Kirkton, which have fine views and fine gardens. Carry on to where the road bends left and there is a cemetery ahead. Here take a path on the right, signed Norham Path, which goes through a kissing gate and down a grassy strip between fields. Move left before the fence and cross a rather awkward stile. Walk down the left side of the field, go through a kissing gate and join the shore path. Continue left to return to the parking area. To visit the abbey, walk up to the narrow road and go ahead for a very short way to the entrance. You cannot see the ruins from the road. There is a little parking at the side of the entrance.

Curlew

Practicals

Type of walk: *A delightful stroll beside the Tay, using the Coastal Path. The return route takes you through pleasing countryside, eventually on high ground above the lower path.*

Distance: 6 miles/9.5km

Time: 3–4 hours

Maps: OS Explorer 371/Landranger 59

Walk 37

Morton Lochs and Tentsmuir Forest

Park in the signed car park at Lundin, south east of Tayport, grid ref 466281. Access this from Tayport, by turning east off the B946 along Maitland Road, following signs to the Dolphin Centre. Turn right at the mini-roundabout and continue down Shanwell Road, past Scotcraig and Fife Works. Go left at the sign for Links Road North and Parking. The car park is on the right.

Tentsmuir Forest stands next to Kinshaldy Beach from where there are fine views across the Firth of Tay. It was planted mainly with Corsican and Scots pine, on salt marsh, in the early 1920s. Much of the forest is a National Nature Reserve. Look out for deer, bats, red squirrels and, off the beach, grey seals hauled out on sand bars. Royalty once hunted the area and shipwrecked sailors and other hapless folk lived here in tents – hence the name.

The **ice house** was used by fishermen to store their salmon in ice, before shipping it south as and when it was required. It was built in 1852 and at that time it stood close to the high water mark. Today it stands much further from the sea as the foreshore moves ever more eastwards. The ice house is home to many natterer bats suiting them well as it remains at the same temperature all the year round.

1 Walk left out of the car park and continue past the Links Store to the crossroads. Turn right, passing 'the Works', remaining on

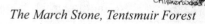

The March Stone, Tentsmuir Forest

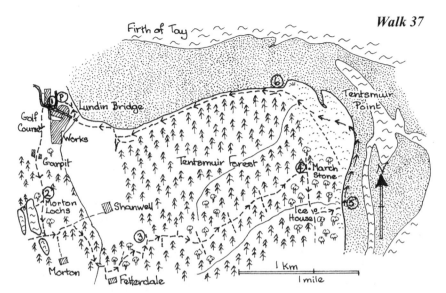

the right pavement, until the road bends right. Cross to walk a track, waymarked a few yards along it. It continues through the middle of Scotscraig golf course and along the way you are reminded to beware of golf balls. The path eventually narrows, beyond a gate, and then keeps to the left side of a house with a high fence and a tall hedge. Go through another gate into the forest and walk ahead. Carry on through a more open area, where many young rowans are thriving and the extra light has encouraged a colourful array of flowers along the edges of the track. Continue on through the forest to come to a larger open area where irises flower in a wetter patch and a large number of purple and white foxgloves thrive.

2 Keep ahead ignoring any side turns until you can take a signed gate, on the right, onto a path leading a short way through pines to a bird hide. Here enjoy the beauty of the first Morton Loch where you might spot heron, little grebe, tufted duck, buzzard and mallard. Return to the main track and walk on to the entrance, on the right, to another bird hide that enables you to overlook the other end of the North Loch. Return to the main track and turn right and after a few steps join a wide sandy track and bear left. Ignore any grassy rides left and right and keep on the wide main track. Go over a cross of tracks and follow the track to a Y-junction. Ignore the left branch to Shanwell and wind right, signed to Fetterdale, still through magnificent pines. Pass a dense shelter belt of sitka spruce and then go off left, at another sign for Fetterdale, along a charming grassy track perfumed at first by

the sweet smelling flowers of several lime trees. Press on to reach a T-junction and turn left.

3 Suddenly you are looking across a pasture to the left, with Tayport in the distance and the Sidlaw Hills beyond. Wind round on the main track, signed to the Ice House, 2 miles. As you continue through more pine forest, look and listen for goldcrests. Ignore more green glades, leading off left and right however tempting. Where the trees lie well back from the track enjoy the flowers, which attract ringlet butterflies and dark green fritillaries, the latter brown but not green though there is a greenish tinge on the hind underwing which gives them the name. At the cross of tracks, go straight on with a wire sculpture of an elephant to the right. At the T-junction and well signposted, walk left to the March Stone on the right; in 1794 it marked the boundary between two lots of salmon fishing rights – March meaning a boundary. At that time the coast was very close to where you are now standing. Here you might spot a roe deer.

4 Return along the track to the junction and go on ahead. A short way along the track you reach the ice house. Just beyond it, turn left and walk through the trees to a gate. Beyond, stroll a sandy path that leads down to the shore of the North Sea. If the tide is out you may wish to walk left along the lovely sands or you may prefer to take the footpath that goes left just before the shore and follow it as it moves away from the sands and keeps in line with huge blocks of concrete, known as 'Dragon's Teeth'. These are tank traps that were placed at high tide level during the 1939-45 war, acting as coastal defence against enemy landing craft.

5 To walk the sands, turn left along the shore and continue. Look out to the sea to the furthest sandbank where you may see dozens of common seals, with last year's pups, all laid out in the sun. You might also see gannets diving for fish. Wind round a small promontory where ringed plovers race across the sand and then look for the wide flat area, with no dunes, where the sea rushes in during the highest tides. Turn left onto this and follow a fairly clear track as it makes its diagonal way towards the far corner of the forest.

Grey Seal

In parts it is very clear and it is a delight to walk over sea milkwort, which might be in delicate flower. Keep well up as you near a huge area of brown shore to come close to the line of tank traps. Here both paths join. Keep on the now clear path as it reaches the corner of woodland to pass through a gate/stile onto a continuing path just above the shore.

6 Follow this lovely path, keeping parallel with the north side of the forest. The vegetation is a delight and in June you might spot purple milk vetch, northern marsh orchid and common wintergreen. The path comes to an end at a sandy bay. Walk ahead over the sand, if the tide is right, or walk round the bay just inside the forest. Rejoin the track when you reach the other side and continue on with maritime heath to the right. Press on along a sturdy path, then turn right to go through a gate and follow the track round to cross Lundin Bridge. Turn right along a narrow reinforced path running along the edge of the salt marsh with the recreation area to your left. At the fork take the left branch to return to the car park.

Common wintergreen

Dabchicks

Practicals

Type of walk: *A lovely walk through varied environments.*

Distance: 8 miles/13km
Time: 4–5 hours
Maps: OS Explorer 371/Landranger 59

Walk 38

Balkello Hill and Auchterhouse Hill

Park in the Balkello Community Woodland car park, grid ref 365385. Access this by leaving Dundee by the A923 in the direction of Coupar Angus. After 2 miles turn right to Kirkton of Auchterhouse. Go sharp right at the end of the village, signed Tealing. After another 2 miles turn left into the large landscaped car park.

Balkello Hill, named Balluderon Hill on the Landranger map, is part of the **Sidlaw range of hills**, which rear up behind Dundee. It sits between Craigowl Hill and Auchterhouse Hill. Craigowl is the hill with the masts and communications dishes on the summit and, Auchterhouse Hill summit is where ancient settlers established a fort hundreds of years ago.

Syd Scroggie was a remarkable man. He was born in 1919 in Canada, his father having emigrated from Fife. The latter fought and was wounded in the 1914–1918 war and died in 1919 due to the after effects of his wounds. His family returned to Scotland and his widow sent their son Syd to school in Edinburgh and then to Dundee where he developed his great love of the hills. He joined the army in 1939 and was blown up two weeks before the war ended. He completely lost his sight and the lower part of his right leg but not his love of the hills. With the help of his friends, later his children, and particularly his second wife

Memorial Cairn, Balkello (or Balluderon) Hill

134

Margaret, he went on to make over 600 ascents. He died in 2006, his fine cairn stands on Balkello Hill.

Walk 38

1 From the car park walk ahead towards the hills and follow the track that bears left, along the edge of a pasture and with woodland on the right. Very soon leave the track and take a similar one that bears right. When part of the trod goes off right keep left on a continuing grassy way. Just before a pylon on your right, climb a narrow path, on the left, up through lush vegetation to pass under the power lines. The way climbs steeply at first through gorse, broom and birch, then eases a little. It climbs steeply again before easing once more. Pause here to look for long tailed tits and then go on to join a wide track, which you cross.

2 Go on up another narrow path to reach more open ground from where you can look back to spot the River Tay. Pass through a small quarried area, go down a dip past an extensive rock face. Climb again but before the path descends once more take a narrow path, left, up through gorse and broom and then into immature Scots pine, with more signs of quarrying. Carry on through birch, then step, right, off the narrow path onto a wide track and walk left uphill, where you might spot a cuckoo at the right time of the year.

3 At a huge pile of slate waste, leave the track and take a good path bearing right, which very soon divides and you need to take the lower one, on the right. Go past a quarried hollow, which is now delightfully colonised with shrubs and flowers; here you are warned to keep away from the dangerous cliffs, caused by quarrying. Carry on up through heather which now covers the whole of the hilltop and is a wonderful sight in August. When you spot the fine summit cairn, engraved with Syd Scroggie's name, turn left up a little path to it. On the top of the cairn is a toposcope describing the wonderful panoramic view.

4 Leave by a track through the heather, west, in the direction of Ben Lawers on the toposcope, to join another and descend, left, through heather and broom. The path, rough in places with 'ball-bearing' stones, is interspersed with grassy patches. It soon winds right, with

Auchterhouse Hill ahead, and descends to a col named Windy Gates. Walk left along the grassy path and where it winds left take the right fork at a Y-junction. The way passes through bracken, then birch woodland and on to an open area where it joins a wider track. Turn left. Curve round left in the open area, once an old quarry, with a picnic table on a little hillock to your right and bear left on the tempting wide grassy trod going ahead.

5 Alas, leave it at once and take a narrow path, right, hardly visible through summer grass, and descend gently. Join another wide track and continue right, downhill. Pass through birch woodland and then under the power lines, with a pylon below to the right. Descend the path to wind right round the foot of the pylon and climb the grassy way to join a track coming in on your right, where you drop left through more woodland. At the T-junction turn left and keep ahead through a drystone wall, where there are two seats. Continue on the reinforced way to return to the car park.

Cuckoo

Practicals

Type of walk: *A lovely walk with a feeling of 'away from it all'. It is not well signposted and the relevant Explorer map shows many paths. Keep alert for the narrow paths, going off left and up, which cross two good tracks, the second one leading you to the summit.*

Distance: 3 miles/5 km
Time: 2–3 hours
Maps: OS Explorer 380/ Landranger 54

Crombie Country Park

Park in the car park at Crombie Country Park, grid ref 528403, where there is a small charge. To access this follow the A92 which runs from Dundee to Arbroath. Turn left onto the B9128 at Muirdrum and continue to the intersection with the B961, where you turn left. After ½ mile/1km turn right into the park entrance.

In 1866, a reservoir was built at a former quarry in Crombie Den; but Crombie Loch was unable to provide enough water for Carnoustie's needs, and it ceased functioning in 1981. It is now part of **Crombie Country Park**, opened in 1983.

A short horseshoe detour on the right reveals the site of a **Cist** – a stone burial chamber built by the Beaker people around 4000 years ago.

Cist burial chamber, Crombie Reservoir

1 Leave the car park keeping to the right of a small hut used as an information cabin. This is where you pay your parking fee. Walk on along a good path through birch woodland and then pines, from where you can look down on Crombie Den through which hurries the outflow from the loch. Carry on to reach the edge of the loch where you will want to pause to enjoy the fine view up the lovely stretch of water. Walk right over the long bridge across the outflow and go on across the dam. On its steep slope woody cranesbill grows in profusion. Press on around the Anglers' jetty and then on through pines with a glorious array of ferns. From here you have little glimpses of the loch. Then continue through deciduous woodland, always on a good path, and in summer serenaded by the many blackbirds that nest here. Take some of the little paths on the left through the trees to the side of the water.

2 Towards the foot of the loch aquatic pink per-sicaria grows densely over the surface of the water. To visit the fascinating Cist site look for the signed path, on the right, that leads to it. This eventually leads you back to the main path. Wind on around the foot of the loch to cross a bridge over a stream where water crowfoot and watercress flower. The path brings you near to a road. Ignore the exit to it and follow the path, left, which soon leads away from it and takes you on an open area at the foot of the loch. Turn right if you wish to look at an old croft with some interesting farm machinery, or left to continue along the other side of the loch. Here the shallow water is covered with horsetails where, in the middle of the plants is a little pool where greylag geese brood their young. Walk on beside the open water, until the path moves away to the side of more Scots pine. A sign directs you left through the dark plantation to a bird hide overlooking the open water once more. On the opposite side is a man-made sand martin bank with holes much used at the right time of the year. Look also for heron, mallard, and coot. Return to the path and carry on, left, from where you can see more of the loch.

3 Then at the end of the woodland, step up onto a fine, long embankment to walk beside the loch. From here you might spot heron, common sandpiper, and swans with cygnets. Stroll this lovely way. Enjoy the fine reflections and the quiet. This brings you back to the track, which you follow ahead to the car park.

Practicals

Type of walk: *A pleasing level walk on good paths, with much to see and hear.*

Distance: 3 miles/5km

Time: 2 hours

Maps: OS Explorer 382/Landranger 54

Walk 40

Seaton Cliffs, Arbroath

Park in the parking area at the end of Victoria Park, grid ref 659412, overlooking the sea and with the public toilets close by. Access this from Arbroath town, where it is well signposted, by an unclassified road, east, off the A92.

The lovely path takes you along the fantastic sandstone **Seaton Cliffs** and is managed by Scottish Wildlife Trust. It runs all the way from the start at Victoria Park to the northern end of Carlingheugh Bay. The seashore and cliffs throughout the 17th century, and later, were once the haunt of **smugglers** but in the early 18th century the Customs Officers' sloop, the Princess Caroline, based at Arbroath, patrolled this area and smuggling along the coast came to an end.

1 Walk to the end of the of the parking area and take the tarred way, climbing easily, to the signpost at the top of a cliff, enjoying the myriad of wild flowers along the banking on either side. Ignore the left turn that returns you to the town. Go ahead along the good cliff top path to wind round a geo, an inlet cut by the sea. Enjoy the dramatic views down to the many rocks at the foot of the high red sandstone cliffs where, on tiny ledges of the sheer sides, kittiwakes nest. Pass the sandstone arch of Needle E'e, where helmeted young people jump from a height into the boiling sea, and then on past more weird sandstone formations.

The Deil's Heid, Seaton Cliffs

Ignore a metal kissing gate at the head of a vast canyon, Dickmont's Den, giving access to an extensive area of polythene tunnels where soft fruit is grown. Once the Den was great smuggling territory. Carry on along the edge of the canyon where common vetch and purple milk vetch grow together in the shallow banking. As you continue on along the cliff path look ahead to see Deil's Heid (the devil's head), a bulbous sea-stack with sloping slab rocks at its foot.

Purple milk vetch

2 There are seats along this exciting cliff path, where you can pause in safety to enjoy the sea birds, the wonderful array of flowers, the restless sea and its fantastic cliffs. Follow the path as it begins to wind along the edge of enormous Carlingheugh Bay. Stay on the cliff path and as you enter the trees above Seaton Den, then cross a long wooden footbridge over a very deep ravine through which flows a feeder stream. Descend steadily into the Den and cross the burn on convenient stones, or wade if this is not possible, to reach a signpost. The Coast path is signed to the right but this walk goes straight ahead, following a sign for Arbroath Path Network. Don't take the obvious path along the bottom of the glen. The path you need climbs gently through a groove to join a path at the top. Turn left at the waymarks and walk along the top of Seaton Den. Go down

Walk 40

gradually and cross or wade the burn and then climb gently into an avenue of beech trees.

3 Walk up this delightful way on a good path through the beech and then some gorse. Eventually you can hear the occasional noise of traffic ahead. Just before you reach what is really a quiet road, turn left into a shelterbelt of trees, on the left, which runs parallel with the road. The path is clear and pleasing to walk through the deciduous woodland. After ½ mile/1km, the path apparently stops. Move left for a few steps and go on along a very narrow path outside the trees with a barbed wire fence to your left. Soon the path swings, right, across a lush area, to join a good path through the continuing shelterbelt once more to reach the side of a short, wide, access road to a holiday village. Turn left.

4 Beyond the entrance to the village, the way continues as a pleasing hedged track for another ¼ mile/0.5km and brings you to a road at East Seaton. Turn right and then almost immediately left along a wide track that can be muddy, after rain, caused by the movement of heavy vehicles. The track goes on beside acres of poly-tunnels where strawberries are grown. Follow the way as it eventually winds round left and, a short way along, turn right to walk a few steps to the metal kissing gate at Dickmont's Den, ignored on your way earlier. Turn right and follow the cliff path back to Victoria Park.

Kittiwakes

Practicals

Type of walk: *A spectacular cliff walk, followed by a delightful return through woodland and a long shelterbelt of trees. Take care along the cliffs in windy weather.*

Distance: 5½ miles/9km
Time: 3–4 hours
Maps: OS Explorer 382/ Landranger 54

Walking Scotland Series
from Clan Books

MARY WELSH AND CHRISTINE ISHERWOOD have completed this series of guides covering the whole of Scotland's mainland and principal islands.

Full list of volumes available:

1. WALKING THE ISLE OF ARRAN
2. WALKING THE ISLE OF SKYE
3. WALKING WESTER ROSS
4. WALKING PERTHSHIRE
5. WALKING THE WESTERN ISLES
6. WALKING ORKNEY
7. WALKING SHETLAND
8. WALKING THE ISLES OF ISLAY, JURA AND COLONSAY
9. WALKING GLENFINNAN: THE ROAD TO THE ISLES
10. WALKING THE ISLES OF MULL, IONA, COLL AND TIREE
11. WALKING DUMFRIES AND GALLOWAY
12. WALKING ARGYLL AND BUTE
13. WALKING DEESIDE, DONSIDE AND ANGUS
14. WALKING THE TROSSACHS, LOCH LOMONDSIDE AND THE CAMPSIE FELLS
15. WALKING GLENCOE, LOCHABER AND THE GREAT GLEN
16. WALKING STRATHSPEY, MORAY, BANFF AND BUCHAN
17. WALKING AROUND LOCH NESS, THE BLACK ISLE AND EASTER ROSS
18. WALKING CAITHNESS AND SUTHERLAND
19. WALKING THE SCOTTISH BORDERS AND EAST LOTHIAN
20. WALKING AYRSHIRE, RENFREWSHIRE AND LANARKSHIRE
21 WALKING FIFE, THE OCHILS, TAYSIDE AND THE FORTH VALLEY

Books in this series can be ordered through booksellers anywhere. In the event of difficulty write to
Clan Books, The Cross, DOUNE, FK16 6BE, Scotland.

For more details, visit the Clan Books website at
www.walkingscotlandseries.co.uk